I0130626

Sociological Readings and Re-readings

Published in 1996, this book comprises a number of essays by Paul Atkinson in which he reflects on processes of reading and writing in the social sciences. Topics covered include: ethnographers' 'confessions', an analysis of the style of Erving Goffman, a reflection of his own experiences of re-reading work, and a discussion of the challenges of reading an alien discipline.

This book was originally published as part of the *Cardiff Papers in Qualitative Research* series edited by Paul Atkinson, Sara Delamont and Amanda Coffey. The series publishes original sociological research that reflects the tradition of qualitative and ethnographic inquiry developed at Cardiff. The series includes monographs reporting on empirical research, edited collections focussing on particular themes, and texts discussing methodological developments and issues.

Sociological Readings and Re-readings

Paul Atkinson

Routledge
Taylor & Francis Group

First published in 1996
by Avebury, Ashgate Publishing Limited

This edition first published in 2018 by Routledge
2 Park Square, Milton Park, Abingdon, Oxon, OX14 4RN
and by Routledge
711 Third Avenue, New York, NY 10017

Routledge is an imprint of the Taylor & Francis Group, an informa business

© 1996 Paul Atkinson

Publisher's Note
The publisher has gone to great lengths to ensure the quality of this reprint but points out that some imperfections in the original copies may be apparent.

Disclaimer
The publisher has made every effort to trace copyright holders and welcomes correspondence from those they have been unable to contact.

A Library of Congress record exists under LCCN: 95083042

ISBN 13: 978-0-8153-8481-6 (hbk)
ISBN 13: 978-1-351-20223-7 (ebk)
ISBN 13: 978-0-8153-8482-3 (pbk)

Sociological Readings and Re-readings

PAUL ATKINSON
School of Social and Administrative Studies
University of Wales, Cardiff

Avebury

Aldershot • Brookfield USA • Hong Kong • Singapore • Sydney

Published by
Avebury
Ashgate Publishing Limited
Gower House
Croft Road
Aldershot
Hants GU11 3HR
England

Ashgate Publishing Company
Old Post Road
Brookfield
Vermont 05036
USA

British Library Cataloguing in Publication Data

Atkinson, Paul
    Sociological Readings and Re-readings –
    (Cardiff Papers in Qualitative Research; Vol.4)
    I. Title II. Series
    301
ISBN 1 85628 578 2

Library of Congress Catalog Card Number: 95-83042

Contents

Acknowledgements

I am as always grateful to Sara Delamont, for her tireless support and encouragement over the years, and for her help in preparing this collection of essays. She has made a contribution to everything I have been able to write and I can detect her influence throughout this volume.

For permission to reprint versions of the following papers I am grateful to the publishers. 'Supervising the text' first appeared in *International Journal of Qualitative Studies in Education*, 4 (1991) 161-174 and is reprinted here with the permission of Taylor and Francis; 'Goffman's poetics' was first published in *Human Studies*, 12 (1989) 59-76, and is reprinted with the permission of Kluwer; 'The ethnography of a medical setting' first appeared in *Qualitative Health Research* , 2 (1992) 451-474, and is reprinted here with permission of Sage. 'At Man's Best Hospital and the Mug'n'Muffin' first appeared (slightly shorter) in N.P. McKeganey and S. Cunningham-Burley (eds) *Enter the Sociologist* (Avebury 1987) and is included here with the publisher's permission.

For their help in wodprocessing various drafts and versions of these essays I am especially grateful to Liz Renton and Pauline Donovan, who have grappled with my handwriting with unfailing cheerfulness.

1 Introduction

In this short volume I have allowed myself the luxury of putting together a number of essays - some previously published, others appearing here for the first time. Those that have been published in earlier versions were not all placed in very accessible publications and it is unlikely that any reader would have encountered more than one or two of them before. The unpublished essays were prepared originally as conference presentations. All have been revised to a greater or lesser degree since their original composition.

Together, the papers go back over a number of years. I began writing about sociological texts and sociological composition in the late 1970s, and the first of my publications in that area appeared in 1982. A much revised and up-dated version appears as the first chapter of this volume. When I first began to explore those issues there was virtually no literature to draw on. For instance, when - at about the same time - Martyn Hammersley and I were writing the first edition of *Ethnography: Principles in Practice* (1983) there were no models when we prepared the chapter on writing an ethnography. We relied heavily on our commonsense reading of ethnographic monographs, our own experiences, and some insights gained from literary criticism. The result was a fairly robust guide for our readers, but in the absence of a literature with which and against which to shape our ideas, our views were necessarily somewhat rudimentary.

Since those early contributions, of course, the position has quite reversed. Far from a paucity of material creating a problem, one's difficulty is now a result of the sheer volume of published commentary and analysis. The writing and reading of the human and social disciplines is now a major genre of scholarly literature in its own right. Were one to try to review it in its entirety, then it would need all of this short book and more to do so. Even the production and interpretation of ethnographic texts (in anthropology, sociology and cognate fields) has now generated a substantial body of analysis.

1

I have contributed to some aspects of that literature, including two previous books, *The Ethnographic Imagination* (1990) and *Understanding Ethnographic Texts* (1992). Several of the essays included here were developed in parallel with those monographs, as were others not reprinted here, which included a number of collaborations with Sara Delamont. Those co-authored papers have been collected together elsewhere under the title *Fighting Familiarity* (Delamont and Atkinson 1995). It is not my desire to recapitulate all of my previous contributions: the essays collected here make their own contributions to the literature, I hope.

They begin with a general essay on ethnographic texts. This is by no means a comprehensive synopsis, but it provides some general observations on the mutual influences of ethnography and literary styles. In particular it focuses on the tradition stemming from the sociological and literary mileu of Chicago. This theme - the literary antecedents and analogues of the Chicago School of sociology - has recently been addressed by Cappetti (1993) among others, and the essay is brought up to date with the inclusion of her work. The themes reflected in the treatments of the Chicago School and its legacy have a particular piquancy. For they show that an interplay between textuality and sociology is by no means a recent development, though its forms and degree of selfconsciousness have changed.

Indeed, in tracing these historical antecedents I argue that recent and contemporary commentaries, often derived from feminist, poststructuralist and postmodernist tendencies, construct unnecessarily sharp distinctions between the past and the present in characterising ethnography, both as a method and as a genre. I suggest that a sensitivity to the textual or rhetorical forms of ethnography (indeed, of any sociological representation) is in direct line of descent from symbolic interactionism. By no means all the urban ethnographers who have carried on the programme of research foreshadowed in Chicago have done so with the explicit aim of developing symbolic interactionism. Nevertheless, a certain style of ethnography and a broadly interactionist sociology have been closely associated. I recognise that in its origins, urban ethnography was somewhat insouciant about its own forms, while being sensitive to other forms of cultural representation. Equally, however, I suggest that a contemporary preoccupation with such forms is not a rupture but a continuation - perhaps even a completion - of a symbolic interationist ethnography. In that first essay, then, I recapitulate some themes that will probably be familiar to some readers at least. I outline how considerations of textuality arise once one pays close attention to the forms of representation that characterise ethnographic reading and writing. I suggest that form and content, style and substance, are linked inextricably in the construction and interpretation of ethnographic texts.

These themes are taken up in the second essay. Here I pay much more attention to contemporary positions regarding textuality and ethnographic inquiry. I try to suggest two things. First, I am entirely sympathetic to a variety of 'textualism' in the treatment of ethnography itself. I argue, indeed,

2

that our texts of sociology or anthropology are, in important sense, possible by virtue of their intertextual relations with other texts (not necessarily just other ethnographies). Our representations of the social world are not innocent or neutral. They necessarily share rhetorical or discursive features with other textual representations. It would be remarkable - and the texts would probably be incomprehensible - were that not so. To that extent, therefore, I suggest that one can think of ethnographies as parodies or even pastiches of other texts: textual data, other ethnographies, other genres (factual and fictional). I then use this this as a point of departure to explore the varieties of alternative genre and rhetoric that may be available to authors and readers. One can readily recognise that once the essentially conventional nature of ethnographic reporting is recognised, then the way is opened up for a diversity of representations and textual forms. This, indeed, has been the message of commentators from various perspectives, most notably feminist and poststructuralist. While welcoming the vigorous proliferation of textual forms and experiments, the essay concludes by calling for a responsible and principled approach to textual work.

These themes are addressed once more in a slightly different way in the third of the essays. Here I turn to the responsibility of academics in sponsoring and appraising ethnographic work. I try to think about how a renewed selfconsciousness about textual forms and conventions may place new and greater burdens on people like graduate students and their academic advisers. We need, I suggest, to encourage skills of reading and writing in the acquisition of craft knowledge among social scientists. We need to recognise that such craft-based awareness will not make the work of research and reportage any easier. Indeed, the greater our selfconsciousness and the more acute our perception of conventional forms, the more complex our analytic and literary work may need to become. Once more I emphasise the fact that heightened critical awareness must impose more responsibilities.

These essays on ethnographic work are completed by an essay on the reading, rereading and analysis of ethnographic data. Here I comment on techniques of reading and rereading fieldnotes. It is based on my own experience of reading my fieldnotes after the passage of time. I reflect on how I seem to have read my data on two separate occasions. I went back to fieldnotes some twenty years after I had first constructed them. That was not because I had no fresher data, nor because I could think of nothing else to do with my time. It was undertaken as an explicitly methodological exercise. Our collective interest in the texts of ethnographic work, especially among anthropologists, has now given rise to some explicit attention to the construction and interpretation of fieldnotes. We know that they are generated through acts of writing and composition. We know too, of course, that our 'analyses' are not mechanistic processes but acts of reading and interpretation. It is, therefore, appropriate to include some attention to field data in the context of these essays on reading and rereading.

3

The two essays that follow are addressed to one specific genre of ethnographic text. Many ethnographers, sociological and anthropological, have contributed to a particular genre by writing autobiographical accounts of their experiences 'in the field'. Such autobiographical accounts, which Van Maanen has called 'confessionals', contrast with the standard, less personal accounts of the research and the results that are to be found in the vast majority of monographs, dissertations and journal articles. Here I reprint one of my own autobiographical accounts, based on fieldwork in the United States, in which I also reflect briefly on how and why authors like me come to write such accounts of the personal side of research. This reflective theme is carried forward in the essay that follows. There I undertake a more sustained analysis of confessionals. I do not attempt to produce a comprehensive review of all possible confessional tales of the field. I concentrate on the work of sociologists working in urban settings. My main purpose there is to show that despite their autobiographical and confessional nature, they are thoroughly conventional in character. Even when we are, or think we are, at our most personal, we represent ourselves in accordance with the patterns of a genre. Textual devices and recurrent motifs provide shared frameworks for the ceation of shared experience. Confessions may reflect different conventions from the classic style of realist ethnographic writing, but they are conventional for all that. There will clearly be scope to extend this analysis once more to other sub-genres of confessional account. I suspect that broadly similar themes and forms will be found.

My interests in sociological style and genre are not confined exclusively to ethnographies and ethnographic methodology, narrowly defined. One of my arguments is that a great deal of sociological analysis and argument are carried forward implicitly. How an author writes about the social world may convey her or his sociology more powerfully and more persuasively than explicit propositions. Such a perspective can be demonstrated through a close reading of one author. The next essay therefore takes a careful look at the work of Erving Goffman. In one sense, of course, he is an easy case. There is widespread recognition of the significance of Goffman's style, and I am by no means the only commentator to have examined Goffman's characteristic modes of written expression.. I do not offer a systematic survey of all of Goffman's published output, and I pay most attention to some of the best known works. This is primarily an exercise in the close rereading of familiar texts.

In a contrasting chapter I turn to the reading of a thoroughly unfamiliar corpus of work. I comment on my reading of a restricted number of texts in health economics, from the perspective of a sociologist of medicine. I thus approach the texts as an outsider when it comes to the discipline of economics. There was a very specific reason for such an exercise in reading and for the original preparation of that hitherto unpublished essay. There was a joint conference between sociologists of medicine and health economists, sponsored by the respective professional groups in the United Kingdom. In the course of the conference pairs of sociologists and economists examined topics of mutual interest. There were, in addition, two parallel opening keynote addresses by a sociologist and an economist. Each was required to comment on the other's discipline, and in preparation each read a specified, representative selection of literature from the other side. I was asked to be the sociologist, and so I read a number of works by health economists, taken from the reading list provided. (Several other sociologists had taken the better part of valour before I was approached and was persuaded to tackle the task.) It proved to be far from easy to construct a coherent argument or even a succinct commentary on the material. Somehow, throughout that conference - which itself gained a certain notoriety - the economists found it easier to form a view of sociology and sociologists than the reverse. My opposite number felt able to comment on the sociology he had read with far greater confidence than I was able to muster in my reading of health economics. Indeed, the overwhelming sense that I came away with, and that I tried to convey in my paper, was that of the *strangeness* of the other discipline. It was not, I think, simply a failure of understanding on my part (although I am sure I was not able to comprehend the texts in the ways the economists could). Rather, I was struck more forcibly and more generally by the 'strangeness' of the work I read. Consequently, my original presentation dwelt on the phenomenology of trying to read an unfamiliar discipline. As is the case with some of my other essays, the original paper predated much of the explosion of scholarly work on the rhetoric of the natural and social sciences. I was at the time feeling my way towards a view of how a discipline like economics is constructed by its distinctive conventions of writing and reading. The essay included here has been updated to some small extent, but I have not rewritten it entirely. I try to avoid creating the impression that its inspiration came directly out of literature that in reality postdated it. At the time of its original presentation, for instance, McCloskey's important work on the rhetoric of economics (McCloskey 1985) had not been published in book form, but reference is now made to it in this revised version. The essay is included in this collection partly because it helped me to reflect on the phenomenology of reading as I developed my own more general work on sociology and texts. The original paper was never published for various reasons, not least because of the schism that appeared in the conference itself. The sociologists seemed unable to shake the faith of the economists, who thus appeared to be stubborn and smug, while the economists remained sceptical about the contributions of sociology. The problem was compounded by the further (all too familiar) trait among the sociologists: unlike the economists they seemed to have little faith in their *own* discipline. One consequence of these clear differences and the attendant process of polarisation was the publication in a special issue of the journal *Social Science and Medicine* of the presentations by the health economists alone. Obviously I must have helped to make that supposedly interdisciplinary event such a non-meeting of minds. I like to think that at least I did so in a rather

5

more imaginative way than most of the other culprits. The essay makes more sense in the context of other work on reading and writing any way. It was like a fish on a bicycle among the health economists, and indeed among some of the less reflexive among the sociologists, just as I was clearly a stranger among the economists' texts.

Finally, in a brief concluding essay (like this Introduction, of course, written specifically for this collection), I reflect on the current state of the art. There is now a bewildering variety of approaches to the examination of sociological and anthropological texts. some standpoints are associated with quite wild and woolly thinking, and this is an area in which enthusiasm can be dangerous. I try to suggest a balance between the licence to experiment and the mandate of scholarly responsibility - a theme that recurs in various guises throughout these essays.

2 Ethnography in perspective

Introduction

In this essay I shall explore some of the parallels between one tradition in ethnographic research, associated with symbolic interactionism, and literary conventions or precedents. I shall suggest that there was something of a contradiction between the epistemological stance of interactionist ethnography on the one hand, and the conventional means used to represent it on the other. I shall suggest that the pragmatist tradition within symbolic interactionism has always stressed the exploratory nature of a social world in constant flux. Neither social order nor social identities are stable and unitariy. The view of incomplete and uncertain knowledge may be contrasted with the implicit assumptions of realist reportage, explicitly derived from realist fiction, that has been used to construct ethnographic texts. I shall then go on to suggest, however, that it is not necessary to invoke recent and fashionable perspectives - such as postmodernism - in order to recognize that issue. A close attention to textual forms may be seen as an extension of symbolic interactionism rather than a radical break with the past.

Symbolic interactionism: theory and method

Symbolic interactionism is marked by a high degree of coherence, in terms of the relationship between theory and method, and an impressive tradition of theory and research. As Williams remarked, 'the productivity of symbolic interactionist research compares favourably with any theory/research tradition in sociology, and its integration of theory and method through particular styles of research makes possible a coherence that other recent developments will lack' (Williams 1976). This coherence is not without its internal contradictions, however, and one major contradiction willl form the main focus for much of this essay. Much of that coherence, moreover, has

7

been implicit. Rock (1979) referred to symbolic interactionism as an 'understated sociology'. To a considerable extent, it has been embodied in an oral tradition, shared among its adherents, rather than fully expressed in explicit, axiomatic statements of general theory. It has been more important for symbolic interactionism to be demonstrated through empirical research rather than programmatic statements.

It is certainly the case that symbolic interactionism has many loose ends in its theoretical and methodological traditions. There are very good grounds for that in the premisses on which interactionism was established. As Rock (1979:70) puts it, knowledge as a process of experiencing

> suggests that men [sic] cannot grasp essences or absolutes because there are no such fixed noumena. Reality shifts as men build it up in their transactions with nature and with each other. It shifts as their problems and vantage points change. Indeed, there is no one reality but a pluralistic universe in which perspectives jar or become amassed. The result is indeterminacy, and abandonment for the quest for the phantom of certainty and its susurpation by an acknowledgement of openness. Knowledge can never be complete or confident.

Interactionism rejects any suggestion that a logic of inquiry can guide research 'independent of the obdurate character of the empirical world to which the methodology is to apply' (Blumer 1969:27). As Williams (1976) discusses, symbolic interactionism posits the primacy of ontology over epistemology. In Herbert Blumer's deceptively simple conclusion:

> Respect the nature of the emprical world and organise a methodological stance to reflect that respect. That is what symbolic interactionism strives to do. (Blumer 1966)

The use of ethnographic research methods represents one major attempt to achieve this congruence between ontology and epistemology, between theory and research. There is a family resemblance between interactionism's construction of the social actor and of social action on the one hand, and on research as an activity on the other. Blumer (1969:2) presents the fundamental concerns of symbolic interactionism in terms of three major premises:

> Human beings act towards things on the basis of the meaning that things have for them.
> The meaning of such things is derived from, or arises out of the social interaction that one has with one's fellows.

These meanings are handled in, and modified through, an interpretative process used by the person in dealing with the things he [sic] encounters.

In common with cognate versions of interpretative sociology, symbolic interactionism regards the social world as essentially a world constituted through meaningful and intentional action. Such meanings and definitions are essentially processual: they are created and recreated through social interaction. They are repeatedly subject to redefinition or reaffirmation. Likewise, actors' selves and identities are processual: they are to be thought of as processes of becoming rather than as stable entitites. The metaphor of negotiation is often used to capture the processes of social interaction whereby meanings are socially generated and shared, and whereby a social order - itself a matter of process - is constantly regenerated. Such processes never reach a final resting point. The outcome of negotiation is further negotiation in the light of new definitions and perspectives. Order, meanings and identities are emergent phenomena. Thought of from such a perspective then, the social world is a highly precarious accomplishment, subject to repeated flux.

Central to the interactionist programme is an emphasis on the reflective capacity of the human actor, made possible by the uniquely human attribute of language and dialogue. By virtue of linguistic competence, the human actor is able to act reflectively, being simultaneously the subject of his or her actions, and an object of his or her own knowledge. It is through this same capacity that the human actor is able to take the role of the other, perceiving other actors as the subjects of their own actions as well as the object of one's perceptions and interpretations. Social interaction is thus symbolic interaction, through which engage in mutual interpretation and self-monitoring, through which those actors 'fit their respective lines of action to one another'.

It is therefore entirely congruent with the symbolic interactionist conception of social life that its methods of inquiry themselves should be based on social interaction and that the discoveries of such inquiry should be regarded as emergent phenomena. That is, as Glaser and Strauss (1967) put it, interactionist work aims at the discovery of 'grounded theory'.Social realities are mapped through their active exploration by a social actor, rather than being amenable to the imposition of predetermined theoretical schemes. Indeed, the emphasis on such active engagement with the world renders the phrase *research work* especially appropriate. It is work, like any other.

This is the rationale that informs the use of ethnographic research methods in the interactionst tradition. It has given rise to an impressive corpus of empirical research on a wide range of topics and settings in twentieth-century societies. Major contributions have been made to the study of urban life, deviance, education, medicine and psychiatry, work and occupations. Although diverse techniques have been drawn on under the rubric of symbolic interactionsim, a major component of this research tradition has been *participant observation,* which is itself the characteristic approach of ethnographic fieldwork. Participant observation is the research approach that is most characteristic of the interactionst, ethnographic tradition (Atkinson and Hammersley 1994, Hammersley and Atkinson 1995).

The researcher-as-ethnographer is modelled on the interactionist's view of the social actor and of experience and self-knowledge in the world. This view derives directly from George Herberrt Mead and his adoption of the pragmatist approach to knowledge (Rock 1979:59-101). The actor engages in the process of flux of the natural and social world and through his or her transactions, negotiates social worlds and social selves. Through a constantly developing series of transactions in the world the actor creates and recreates meaning. As Rock (1979:79-80) says of the interactionist homunculus:

> He [sic] is thrust into the role of the archetypal explorer of social settings, a puppet and scout who lays bare the social reality about him. The actor of interactionist anthropoology is tantamount to the identical subject-object navigating the world. His experiences and encounters belong not only to him, they are also the sociologist's and, vicariously, the reader's. The epistemological status of his doings is relatively sure; he is a peripatetic guarantee of authenticity. Matza's deviant, Paul Cressey's taxi-dancer, Donald Cressey's embezzler, Sutherland's professional thief, Marvin Scott's jockey and Becker's marihuana user are assembled and then set free to bring back intelligence about the nature of social life.

In precisely the same manner, the ethnographer navigates and explores the varied surface of diverse social scenes - the backwaters as well as the mainstream. By virtue of his or her acts, of the transactions that are engaged in, the ethnographer recounts the actor's discoveries and self-discoveries. Informants and hosts tell their stories and in turn the ethnographers have their own tales to tell.

The authenticity of ethnographic work stems from the homology between the researcher and the researched, between the subject-matter and the methods, which themselves are grounded in social transactions. While participant observation is the type case of such research methods, the same considerations and rationales apply to other methods of inquiry, such as the ethnographic interview. Whatever analytic and theoretical superstructure may be erected on it, the ethnographer's knowledge rests on his or her lived experience of the form of life to be explored, reconstructed and reported. In the light of the maxims cited above from Blumer, the ethnographer seeks to engage with fellow actors, in selected social settings, in order to engage with and capture the fleeting, shifting fabric of meaning and order as they are generated through social interactions. The researcher 'in the field', then, draws on precisely those social competences and experiences employed by the actors under scrutiny. This is by far the most significant aspect of *participant* observation. The researcher necessarily participates in the sense that that he or she partakes of the same social activity as other actors in accomplishing the research, and in formulating interpretations. This aspect of participation is far more fundamental than any local considerations concerning practical or ethical problems of gaining access to or joining in particular settings.

In order to accomplish this, the fieldworker treads a line between being a stranger and being a member. He or she may approach members of the host culture quite explicitly as an outsider, and in doing so may appear - as Lofland so nicely put it - as an 'acceptable incompetent' (Lofland 1971). In common with any novice or recruit the researcher than attempts to become culturally competent. The initial position of outsider enables one to approach the chosen setting as *anthropologically strange*. The researcher's position is therefore analogous to that of Schutz's 'stranger' (Schutz 1964). The stranger finds his or her taken-for-granted stock of knowledge will not pass muster in the novel situations that he or she encounters. Because the stranger is forced to abandon the natural attitude of 'thinking as usual'. The stranger is thus the archetype of the social inquirer. Likewise, the ethnographer's encounter with strangeness provides the cutting edge of exploration and observation. Alternatively, the fieldworker may find a given setting all-too-familiar (Delamont and Atkinson 1995), and will have to work at estrangement in order to capture the uncertainty or wonder that is a partial prerequisite to inquiry. Here too the natural attitude must be ruptured in order for it to become an object of inquiry as well as, or instead of, being a resource in the conduct of research transactions.

While the ethnographer must learn, then, he or she should not learn so thoroughly or so unreflectingly that the analytic value of estrangement is lost entirely. The reflective capacity of the researcher is paramount, in that the stock of knowledge that is acquired, the experience that is gained, is never accumulated unselfconsciously. Once lost, the existential safety of the natural attitude can never be completely regained: if it is, then the ethnographer is lost, or the research is finished.

Here too, then, the ethnographer's social action parallels exactly that of the interactionist's actor. The action is strategic, it is based on the competence to act towards oneself as an object of reflection. The process of explicit reflection is documented partiucularly well by Geer (1964) in what has now become a classic publication. Geer offers a detailed account, based on analysis of her own notebooks, of her initial reactions during her fieldwork studying American university students. Quite apart from the particular methodological contribution, Geer's paper provides an excellent exemplar of how ethnographers write their fieldnotes, and use them not simply as a record of what was seen and heard but also how the ethnographer conducts a dialogue with and through the notes. Geer provides just one example of how

11

the process of ethnography rests on the fieldworker's capacity to explore and discover the social world, while maintaining the capacity to reflect and comment on that process. As I have remarked already, this presupposes a congruence between the actors and the researcher, and between interactionist theory and method.

There have, however, been tendencies within symbolic interactionism which have seen attempts to graft an alien epistemology onto its underlying premises. Disjunctions between interactionist theory and method have been noted most perceptively by Williams (1976). He points out that in the 'purist' versions of symbolic interactionism - such as Herbert Blumer's - ontology is regarded as taking precedence over epistemology. Blumer's ideal of 'respect' for the empirical world would imply that the researcher engage in exploratory transactions in the world:

> Since action is forged by the actor out of what he [sic] perceives, interprets and judges, one would have to see the operating situation as the actor sees it, perceive objects as the actor perceives them, ascertain their meaning in terms of the meaning they have for the actor and follow the actor's line of conduct as the actor organises it - in short one would have to take the role of the actor and see his world from his standpoint. (Blumer 1966)

The validity of such work would be assured by its faithfulness to the lived experience of social life. It would authentically reflect the process and the indeterminacy of everyday life.

There have, however, been trends within symbolic interactionism aimed at rendering it more respectable in terms of its methodology. This is well exemplified in Denzin's early work, where he attempted to integrate ethnographic methods with more traditional or orthodox approaches. Under the rubric of triangulation it was recommended that research techniques might be combined: participant observation, survey methods, documentary sources, and so on. The problem is, as Williams (1976) notes, that:

> the suggested substitutes for or additions to the participant observation/case-study method are...improper substitutes in that their use implies ontological assumptions incompatible with those of symbolic interactionism as articulated by Blumer.

To a considerable extent, however, the eclecticism of 'triangulation' has become the preferred strategy of many, if not most, sociologists who align themselves with symbolic interactionism. For instance, on the basis of a survey of American interactionists, Reynolds and Meltzer (1973) concluded that it was the deviant minority who relied upon purely ethnographic approaches.

This tension, or potential tension, between theory and method in the interactionist tradition has been remarked on, and partly reflects conscious efforts (whether or not misguided) to render the research more rigorously 'scientific' in conduct. My argument in the rest of this essay will be that there has been an even more fundamental tension or contradiction at the heart of interactionist ethnography which has remained until recently implicit. The argument will be focused on the *writing of ethnography*. In this essay only a preliminary treatment of the topic will be given. Some further, more detailed, considerations will be developed in the following two essays. In order to appreciate the argument at this point it is necessary to re-visit the origins of interactionist ethnography.

The origins of ethnography in interactionism

Historically speaking, there are multiple origins and sources for ethnographic research, and it is not my purpose here to search for the *fons et origo*. Within the sociological canon, one must recognize the influence of Robert Park at Chicago. Park came to the department of sociology at the University of Chicago in middle age, and prior to that his career had included lenghty periods of work as a journalist and a publicist. He helped to bring to sociology in Chicago and to the sociology *of* Chicago the characteristic perspectives of an experienced journalist - a journalist, moreover, who was accustomed to a good deal of firsthand investigation in searching out his stories and his informants. Park himself (cited in Faris 1970: 29) remarked:

> I expect that I have actually covered more ground, tramping about in cities in different parts of the world, than any other living man. Out of all this I gained, among other things, a conception of the city, and the region, not as a geographical phenomenon merely, but as a kind of social organism.

Throughout the development of sociology at Chicago, under the influence of Park, Thomas, their colleagues and students, the ethnographic study of urban life - rather in the manner of Park the journalist - was a central preoccupation. Though as authors like Harvey remind us, it was by no means the only one (Harvey 1987). Whereas in the early decades of this century anthropological fieldworkers were turning outwards to the study of exotic peoples 'elsewhere', the Chicago sociological ethnographers found equally noteworthy forms of social organization and equally striking evidence of social evolution in their own back yard. Or, to be more precise, they found them in the ethnically, economically and culturally varied setting of a rapidly growing and changing metropolitan environment. Like the anthropologists, they too often focused on the exotic: the demi-monde, the deviants and the criminals. As Faris (1970: 65) remarks:

Hobo areas of Chicago were among the least-visited parts of the city, and many readers outside the profession of sociology found the descriptions almost romantically interesting. While ordinary tourists coming to Chicago usually visited parks and museums (and sometimes even the vast stockyards for contrast), it was the University which provided tours for visiting students to such places as Hobohemia, and for a time slumming visits were a fashion among young Chicago intellectuals.

To a considerable extent this preoccupation with underlife in the city and the underdog perspective has remained a characteristic perspective of interactionist inquiry, though by no means to the exclusion of all else. This demi-monde of Chicago city life was also the haunt of many literary figures of the same period. Indeed, the sociological and literary circles overlapped socially, and shared common interests. Moreover, the literary influence on the early urban ethnographers in Chicago is quite clear. Carey (1975), for instance, points out that the sociologists were well acquainted with contemporary literary forms - particularly the realist and naturalistic novel. They were directly influenced by American fictional writing of this sort, and, indirectly, by European realist writing. Carey (1975: 181) quotes the following extract from an interview with Herbert Blumer:

> [some of us] had the opportunity of moving in certain of the literary circles in Chicago that were, so to speak, on the fringes of the 'underworld'. For example, some of our eminent American figures ... Anderson, Bodenheim, Carl Sandburg - they were all there in Chicago in the early twenties. Some of them were clustered down there at the end of 57th Street and the Park. There was a literary colony down there of writers and artists and what not .... And there was also the lower \north Side, where there was a smiliar literary gathering. some of us, I know I was one of them, got into those groups.

The sociologists and novelists of the time shared very similar backgrounds and preoccupations. Cowley (1950) remarks of the literary figures:

> These new men, who would be the first American naturalists were all in some way disadvantaged when judged by the social and literary standards then prevailing. They were not of the Atlantic seaboard, or not of the old stock, or not educated at the right schools,... or not sufficiently respectable in their persons or in their family backgrounds. They were in rebellion against the genteel tradition because, like writers from the beginning of time, they had an urgent need for telling the truth about themselves and there was no existing medium in which they were privileged.

The Chicago sociologists were equally unelevated. The relative newness of their department of sociology and of the city of Chicago itself allowed them to break free from some of the constraints of tradition and good breeding. For novelists and sociologists alike, the city provided endless fascination. Cowley (1950) also remarks of that urban milieu:

> From the beginning they [the novelists] have exulted in the wealth and ugliness of American cities, the splendor of the mansions and the squalor of the tenements. They compared Pittsburgh to Paris and New York to Imperial Rome. Frank Norris thought that his own San Francisco was the ideal city for storytellers; 'Things happen in San Francisco', he said. Dreiser remarked of Chicago, 'It is given to some cities, as to some lands, to suggest romance, and to me Chicago did that hourly .... Florence in its best days must have been something like this to young Florentines, or Venice to the young Venetian.

The sociologists too were absorbed by the flux and diversity of the city of Chicago, which appeared to offer the equivalent of a laboratory - a series of natural experiments in social change, organization and disorganization. The ethnographic approach to urban life was by no means the only method employed by the early Chicago sociologists, but it was distinctive of much of their investigation of the urban mosaic and the variegated social worlds that composed Chicago itself.

The sociologists and the novelists relied on the reportage of social realities in the city, exposing its contrasts and inequalities, displaying its seamy side as well as its socially acceptable face. In so doing they had more than just shared thematic interests. The form and style of their reportage had common roots. Carey (1975: 178) draws attention to this.

> Characteristically, as in the naturalist novel, the reader is introduced to the topic by the writer's looking at, or walking around and observing, the phenomenon as it might appear to a newcomer. This is what Cressey does in 'A Night in a Taxi Dance Hall', what Wirth does as he guides his reader along Maxwell Street, Thrasher as he takes his audience through gangland, and Zorbaugh in his description of the lower North Side 'In the Shadow of the Skyscraper'.

Historically speaking, then, there were close affinities between the development of ethnographic writing in symbolic interactionism and literary forms.

This is the subject of Cappetti's recent exploration of sociological and literary writing in and about Chicago. Cappetti (1993) documents in some detail how certain sociologists and novelists wrote their representations of

15

the city in directly comparable ways. Cappetti chooses to discuss three novelists and their major works. They are not necessarily regarded as major literary figures today, but they are of considerable sociological interest, given their place in the broader cultural milieu in which urban ethnography grew up. She writes about James Farrell and his *Studs Lonigan* trilogy; Nelson Algren and *Never Come Morning*, and Richard Wright's autobiographical two-volume *Black Boy - American Hunger*. She also considers in some detail the sociological contributions of Park, Thomas and Thrasher. She shows how thoroughly the sociological was pervaded by the literary and vice versa. To a considerable extent the ethnographic style of writing has continued to reflect this literary model. Some implications of this are taken up in the remainder of this essay.

Ethnography as text

As we have seen, the origins of ethnographic writing in interactionist sociology are closely linked to forms of non-sociological writing. Park's experience as a practising journalist and the American realist/naturalist novel were highly influential. Yet there would appear to be a marked ambivalence among ethnographers towards such cognate forms of writing. Critics of ethnographic work over the years have often leveled the accusation that it is no better than mere 'journalism', or a sort of inferior novel, or both. And those are criticisms that some ethnographers at least have been sensitive to. They have been at pains to distance themselves from more ephemeral and more literary forms, while expressing alertness to the danger that their work could easily slip into becoming such apparently non-serious products. Ethnography which is slipshod or is felt to be underdeveloped is usually felt to be especially vulnerable to such debasement, and hence such negative evaluation.

On the one hand, then, 'literature' and 'sociology' are conventionally treated as antithetical categories (with journalism and the like occupying an ambivalent, intermediate position. On the other hand, the frequency and ease with which the work of novelists and ethnographers gets compared suggests that - quite apart from historical influences - there are close affinities between the forms of writing. It is not my intention to suggest that writing literature and writing sociology are really the same exercise. But a mere denial of family resemblances does nothing to remove them, and certainly does nothing to resolve any issues related to the forms of sociological inquiry and representation.

I am not suggesting, then, that novels are sociological documents, nor that ethnographic accounts are really works of literature (though some literature can inform sociology, and some sociology can be read as literature). Rather, it is important to recognize as a point of departure that sociology and literature depend on acts of writing and reading, and at that level of representation they may have important affinities. As I shall go on to argue in this essay, the recognition of that point highlights a recurrent problem in the interactionist tradition.

It is my contention that even more explicit attention to textual analysis should be a major preoccupation of ethnographers. Factual sociology and fictional literature are both written and read in accordance with textual and literary conventions. The interpretations that interpretative sociologists, such as interactionists, engage in are achieved very largely through their compositional skills as authors. They are dependent on the kinds of interpretations that readers can draw out of their ethnographies and commentaries. As I began to argue in greater detail elsewhere (Atkinson 1990, 1992) scholarly work such as ethnography (and perhaps especially enterprises like ethnography) depend on their persuasive powers. The construction of sociological or anthropological scholarship in such texts depends rather little on the construction of theoretical propositions. The nomothetic mode is weak in ethnographic writing, and many such texts result in jejune collections of propositions and generalizations. Yet ethnographic publications have considerable force in the canon of texts that constitute a discipline or field of specialization. Generations of sociologists, for instance, have read such key texts as Whyte's *Street Corner Society*. Many probably feel that they have retained a vivid impression of Whyte's reconstruction of everyday life among Italian Americans. Main characters such as Whyte's key informant, Doc, stand out in the memory. Yet most of those who remember the book as a 'classic' would, I suspect, be hard put to it to produce a convincing summary of the book's main contribution to sociological analysis. Like many authors, Whyte achieved his readership and his contribution to the sociological canon through the way he wrote. It is the style of *Street Corner Society*, the ways in which the characters are constructed, in which social action is represented, in which the social setting is evoked, that holds the power of persuasion. We know from recent commentary that Whyte's reconstruction of that setting, those actors, and that culture, is far from exempt from critical commentary. My point here is not that Whyte's monograph has been regarded as a classic contribution because in some general sense he 'got it right', or because his fieldwork was mysteriously better than that of others. Rather, his work has appealed to many academics and their students over the years very largely by virtue of its textual features. It is a commonplace to talk of the 'readability' of authors like Whyte, but it masks an important truth. In Chapter 5 I shall be considering one aspect of Whyte's text in much more detail. (I shall also consider the work of another readable sociologist, Erving Goffman in Chapter 7.) Here I wish simply to assert that what is important is the style of the ethnographic writing. As I discuss from a different perspective in the next chapter, it is important that we be attentive to both the style and the substance of ethnographic reports, but we cannot afford to lose sight of the persuasive power of style and rhetoric even in the context of such scholarly written products. My comments about Whyte can be extended to cover the tradition more closely associated with interactionism, and the more inclusive tradition of ethnographic work inspired by the Chicago School of research. A great deal of that work has achieved its impact through the vivid reconstructions of urban and organizational settings contained in the ethnographies. The social worlds of Chicago itself have, at various times, been graphically conveyed through the published accounts of its sociologists. Social actors - especially the deviant and the margianlised - have been portrayed, often as vivid characters.

On the other hand, there has been something of a historical contradiction between the general epistemological underpinnings of ethnography and the textual forms used to represent that work. For despite interactionism's overt preoccupation with representation, meaning and the significant symbol, ethnographers themselves for many years were remarkably insouciant about the modes of representation that they themselves used to construct accounts of everyday social life. Perhaps in an attempt to escape from the possible jibe that their work was 'mere' literature, on a par with journalism, fiction, travel writing and the like, the writers and readers of ethnography for many years shunned any overt and systematic preoccupations that might have smacked of the aesthetic. At pains to establish that theirs was work of fact rather than fiction, they played down rather than explored any commonalities betweeen their own writing and the texts of others.

Yet they had common interests, historically and in terms of their textual practices. It is for that reason, among others, that we need continuing attention to textual analysis on the part of ethnographers. Both fact and fiction are written and read in the way that they are by virtue of their characteristics as texts, and the conventions of reading that are brought to them. The work of interpretation on the part of sociologists or anthropologists is as much a matter of writing and reading as it is of explicit conceptualisation and theorisation. In part my rationale is foreshadowed by Bruyn (1966: 125) in his discussion of the study of language:

> Language, if left unstudied and unsupervised, may even come to control its own creators. The social scientist may well become like the sorcerer's apprentice; he can weave a magic and a spell with his words about society which can take the shape of myths having a force on the minds of men [sic] not unlike the myths of ancient times. Scientific language, then, must be studied not for its own sake, as in linguistics, but also for other reasons, including the necessity of reducing the magical power that comes with use and misuse of language in social and political life.

Bruyn's agenda goes beyond mine, but we converge on a commitment to the reflexive analysis of sociological and other scholarly writing. Unexamined, such language constructs and conveys powerful messages about society and social science that escape explicit scrutiny. It is, I believe, important for us to avoid a reliance on language and literary conventions as unexamined resources in the reconstruction of social worlds. A recognition of the conventionality and consequentiality of such conventions implies considerable duties and responsibilities for ethnographers. In recent years the textual turn in ethnography has meant a profound loss of innocence for analysts and readers, and - as Bruyn implies - we cannot afford to let the language of sociological or anthropological texts to escape reflection and explicit control. As will be seen in later essays, such a responsibility does not mean a search for forms of representation that are more authentic or more scientific than others. It demands, on the contrary, a disciplined and principled approach to the forms of representation, and an incorporation of such approaches into the craft knowledge of ethnographers in general.

From a different perspective from Bruyn's, Roland Barthes suggested a related rationale. In a discussion of literary criticism Barthes remarks that our taken-for-granted pedagogies encourage students to treat texts as objects of consumption, while their forms and principles of construction are undervalued as topics of study (Barthes 1979). Similar remarks can be made about the texts of sociology or anthropology. Students at all levels are encouraged to consume the works of their discipline. If possible they are taught to be careful consumers arguments are evaluated, ideological implications assessed, relevance is judged, and so on. Students and teachers are encouraged to 'collect' texts. The latest texts are read and reviewed, while all neophytes are required to read and master the sacred texts of the founding fathers. The texts are arranged for consumption in genealogies and typologies (traditions and schools); they are inscribed in ther equivalent of shopping lists and consumer guides (bibliographies and reading lists). Novices are instructed in the use of such written products. The metaphors of such use (even abuse) capture the kind of violence that may be done to them: we talk, for instance, of 'gutting' the literature. When the literature is 'reviewed' in order to produce that uniquely dire textual type, the *review of the literature* it is rendered inert, and the diversity of authors, styles and contents is reduced to the uniformity of a style that approximates to a 'degree-zero' style of lifeless anonymity. Following Barthes, therefore, I want to suggest that we need to treat ethnographies as *texts* rather than *works* (to repeat the distinction that Barthes himself introduced). Barthes proposes a radical distinction between works and texts, thought of in terms of one's approach to them rather than inherent differences in the written products themselves. Conceived of as a work, the literary object is thought of as just that - an object; whereas thought of as a text it is experienced as part of an activity, as a production, in which the reader participates through his or her transactions with the text (Barthes 1979). Our task is not to try to identify two contrasting types of products, to distinguish supposed works from texts. Rather, it is a matter of identifying two contrasting approaches towards reading and writing, and hence of encouraging an approach to ethnographic writing and reading that establishes that genre of scholarly writing as 'texts'.

As I have already said, and as authors like Cappetti remind us, the literary roots of modern ethnography are to be found in the coventions of the realist or naturalistic novel. That form of fiction remains the literary mode with close affinities with ethnography, and a consideration of realism is therefore in order. In pointing to the affinities between ethnographic writing and realist fiction one could be thought to be guilty of little better than tautology. For realism in literary writing may be recognised by its affinity to non-literary forms or genres. As David Lodge put it:

> A working definition of realism in literature might be: the representation of experience in a manner which approximates closely to descriptions of similar experience in nonliterary texts of the same culture. Realistic fiction, being concerend with the action of individuals in time, approximates to history: 'history is a novel which happened; the novel is history as it might have happened' as the Goncourt brothers put it. Thus the realistic novel, from its beginning in the eighteenth century modelled its language on historical writing of various kinds, formal and informal: biography, autobiography, travelogue, letters, diaries, journalism and historigraphy. (Lodge 1977:25)

To do so would be to commit a cardinal error. In the first place we should risk treating the nonliterary writing as if it were an unproblematic mode of representing reality. If one follows Lodge's formulation in a naive or uncritical fashion, then one might treat the realism of, say, travel-books, journalism or biography as self-evident, and hence the realism of fiction as alone deserving critical attention. (I am sure that Lodge himself was not being guilty of such an over-simplification, simply that his statement could be misinterpreted in such a way). For the achievement of their effects, all texts, literary and otherwise, must depend upon their textual arrangements and their rhetorical devices. We must, therefore, be alert to the conventional nature of *vraisemblance* whether it be in fictional or in scholarly discourse.

The conventional character of realism, or vraisemblance has been demonstrated repeatedly in relation to the conventions of scientific and other scholarly styles. In the 1970s and onwards, the 'rhetoric of inquiry' programme has seen a systematic survey of the textual conventions of an almost comprehensive array of natural and cultural disciplines: from history and law to economics, to biology (White 1973, Danto 1985, McCloskey 1985, Bazerman 1988, Myers 1990). Indeed, since Lodge wrote his characterisation of realism it is now easier for us to see the conventionality of the non-literary models themselves, and to recognise the chared conventions of vraisemblance that link the various genres, scholarly and literary. Likewise, as I have describned in considerable detail elsewhere (Atkinson

1990), ethnographers draw on a varied repertoire of rhetorical devices in order to persuade their readers of the authenticity and veracity of their social reconstructions. Equally, readers draw on the same stock of literate knowledge in order to read off the versimilitude of those accounts. (Which is not to say that all readers find all texts equally plausible: clearly some texts 'work' in ways that others do not.) It is not, therefore, enough for an authors simply to declare that an account is an authentic one: the textual conventions in which the text is couched should normally concform to the cultural expectations of realistic representation.

To a considerable extent, then, the conventions of ethnographic reportage have remained rooted in the conventions of realist reportage - whether of a fictional or nonfictional nature. Now, even from within the perspectives of symbolic interactionism, an uncritical adoption of realist *vraisemblance* is problematic. The unmasking of realism is no longer especially fashionable among literary theorists, but it remains pertinent to an informed understanding of ethnographic and cognate work. The reliance on taken-for-granted means to achieve the effects of an authoritative account means that for many years ethnographers shared with their literary counterparts a somewhat unreflective view of their use of language and their textual practices. The historical stance of the realist writer as the apparently passive transcriber of reality is a characteristically 'scientitic' attitude. It serves the end of both positivist and naturalist views of social inquiry. It serves both (despite the fact that they are often treated as antithetical) insofar as both epistemological positions treat language as a transparently neutral medium of representation. As argued in Hammersley and Atkinson (1983, 1995) both positivism and naturalism mistake the nature of the social world and its proper investigation. Both are founded on the essential separation of the Observer and the Observed; but assume an independent reality that can - in principle - be investigated without contamination. On the other hand, a recognition of the constitutive function of language means that one cannot treat it as a transparent medium of representation. Likewise, a sensitive appreciation of social research must dispel the fallacies of vulgar positivism and vulgar naturalism alike. The researcher and the resources of ordinary language are inextricably implicated in the research process and in acts of interpretation and representation. As proposed in Hammersley and Atkinson, therefore, it is necessary to recognize that social research is inescapably *reflexive* in character.

The challenge to realism

In recent years, the vraisemblance of conventional ethnography has come under critical scutiny, however. There have been various inspirations and catalysts for such reappraisals, and they have led to a variety of alternative styles of representation. There is no single, coherent movement here, but influences from wider cultural tendencies - such as poststructuralism, postmodernism, postcolonialism, and feminism - have impinged on the work and texts of ethnographic research. There has been a textual turn in ethnography, leading in some quarters to a belief in a *crisis of representation*. I do not intend to review all the now voluminous literature here (see Coffey and Atkinson 1995 for a selective review). It is, however, useful to outline some of the main perspectives here before going on to suggest that they represent in many instances over-reactions and exaggerated - even immature - responses to the supposed crisis.

Poststructuralism and postmodernism have contributed to a radical questioning of the authority of the text, and of the methods conventionally used to construct it. The conventional ethnographic monograph is seen from this perspective to be a characteristic product of modernity. It enshrines an Enlightenment project of knowledge and representation. The classic ethnography subsumes the potential diversity of societies and cultures under an all-encompassing set of conventions. The social is represented through a single authorial voice, which inscribes a distance between the researcher and the researched, translated into the reporter and the reported. The subjects/objects of the research are, from this point of view rendered 'other', while their own voices are muted. It is the voice of the ethnographer that holds sway. At the same time, the variety of representational forms that are available within the cultural context are ignored and under-represented. The conventional ethnography thus exercises a homogenising effect. In accordance with its modern inspiration, the conventional ethnography seeks *closure*, in seeking to impose a coherent and consistent pattern on the social world. In contrast, the postmodern position seeks to celebrate the variety of representations and voices that co-exist. It avoids the modern certainties of closure, preferring a variegated and interrogative text. Rather than imposing a single stylistic shape on the social world, it promotes the juxtaposition of contrasting styles. Rather than privileging the single, dominant voice of the detached observer, it celebrates a polyvocal text.

Such postmodern stances resonate with particular strands in postcolonial and feminist thought. Critiques such as Said's characterisation of *orientalism* (Said 1978) have helped to contribute to the epistemological and moral crises of disciplines such as anthropology. The detached, invisible but dominant ethnographic author represents not just the enterprise of science, but also that of a Western appropriation of 'the other'. The 'Orient' or the 'Levant' stand here for the multiplicity of 'Others' that have been surveyed and encapsulated in the texts of Western obsevers. Very similar arguments are to be found from feminist standpoints. The contrast of the dominant author of the realist ethnographic tradition *versus* the dominated object of representation recapitulates major themes in feminist epistemology. Hence, for instance, Mascia-Lees *et al.* (1989) outline a project for feminist anthropology in which women are not treated as the voiceless objects of investigation, but as acting subjects with their own voices. In a similar vein, Wolf (1992) suggests that feminst thought in general, and feminist

22

anthropology in particular, is especially given to reflexive, self-critical attitudes, while encouraging the examination of power and discourse. Feminism, she suggests, is necessarily self-conscious concerning its own modes of representation. From a rather different feminist perspective, Clough (1992) also mounts a feminist (if also rather idiosyncratic) critique of realist ethnography, arguing that its conventions have masked the play of power and desire in the ethnographic enterprise.

Some of these issues will emerge again in later chapters. For now it is important to recognise the existance of these various perspectives that converge upon the conventional ethnographic enterprise, and call into question the adequacy of the taken-for-granted ethnography as a textual product. Here I want to suggest that while the general arguments have validity, it is not necessary to abandon all of the traditions of ethnography in consequence.

It is undeniable that a vulgar realism is problematic. For instance, Coward and Ellis (1977) suggest that

> ...realism has as its basic philosophy of language not a production
> (signification being the production of a signified through the
> action of the signifying chain), but an identity: the signifier is
> treated as identical to a (pre-existent) signified. The signifier
> and signified and signifier are not seen as caught up together in
> a process of production, they are treated as equivalents: the
> signifier is merely the equivalent of its pre-established concept.
> It seems as though it is not the business of language to establish
> this concept, but merely to express or communicate it. (p. 47)

Now the historical failure of interactionist ethnography to treat adequately the language of its own accounts is particularly striking, given the centrality of language in interactionist epistemology. It is, after all, central to the interactionist tradition that it is precisely the symbolic function - the significant symbols of which language is the main example - that permits the distinctively human capacity of reflexivity. Language is thus privileged as the means whereby the social or the cultural are constructed. The fundamental model of the interactionists' view of social life and social order is that of conversation: the conversation between the *I* and the *Me* and the conversation between the *Self* and the *Other*. Rock (1979) summarises it in this way:

> The forms of language mediate the workings of consciousness,
> the self and social interchange. In turn, those forms provide
> symbolic interactionism with its own logic of explanation.
> Society is held to emerge from discourse and symbolisation. The
> metaphors which phrase that vision borrow heavily from the

imagery of everyday speech. Interactionism portrays social life as
an ongoing series of conversational encounters. (p. 116)

It is not the case that interactionism has failed to cope with language only in
the context of ethnographic writing. Despite its overt importance, language
has been poorly theorised in the interactionist tradition for the most part.

On the other hand, serious attention to language and to texts of
representation need not constitute a major break with the central tenets of
interactionist sociology. As I have just indicated, language is central to the
interactionist view of society and social action. That rests not just on the
recognition that language is an important medium or vehicle for social
meanings and negotiations. It is fundamental to interactionst episetemology
that language is *constitutive*. Far from being a neutral means of
communication, language is a 'thick' medium of semiosis and therefore
worthy of attention in its own right. There is, therefore, nothing inherently
revolutionary in turning that attention to the examination of ethnographers'
own uses of language in the construction of their own analyses.

Although a good many commentators claim a crisis of representation as a
consequence of a renewed self-consciousness on the part of ethnographers,
there is in my opinion no need to panic, and no need to proclaim major
epistemological ruptures. If ethnographers occupy themselves with problems
of how social realities are socially produced or constructed, then it is self-
evident that they must recognise their own work in constructing (by writing
or by other means) their own versions of social worlds. This is an extension
of the basic rationales of ethnographic inquiry, rather than a threat to it. It is
not necessary to look only to the criticisms from feminists or postmodernists
(illuminating though they are) in order to explore the textual or rhetorical
conventions that have inspired ethnographers, nor to suggest alternative
modes of representation. It is not a necessary corollary of interactionist
sociology or social psychology that the ethnography should be constructed
from a single narrative viewpoint, for example. Indeed one could argue that,
despite the historical converrgence of interactionist ethnography and realist
writing, their combination was contrary to the fundamental tenets of
interactionist work. The urban sociology that gave rise to the classic texts of
Chicago and their derivatives, were, perhaps, insufficiently faithful to
interactionsm itself.

In the chapters that follow, therefore, I shall be examining various sites of
textual practice in sociology, with a primary (but not exclusive) focus on
ethnographic texts. I shall take account of the critiques that exist from
beyond the narrower confines of interactionist sociology, and I shall not be
attempting to reassert a vulgar realism. On the other hand, I shall not be
advocating a fashionable Angst concerning the very possibilities of
ethnographic representation. I believe that it remains possible to *use* textual
conventions in disciplined and principled ways, in order to produce
authoritative and scholarly accounts. It remains an important task for use to

keep under scrutiny that limits of scholarly conventions, and to avoid the uncritical use of any set of representational conventions. We must always be alert to their very conventionality, but that need not prevent us from engaging with the social world and with the textual domain in order to produce scholarly work. The fact that it need not conform to earlier models is no reason to abandon the search for appropriate modes of representation. I regard such work as a natural extension of the reflexive enterprise in interationism and in ethnography.

3 Ethnography: parody and pastiche

Introduction

The village of Topos is reached by bus from Chania, the main town of Western Crete. The visitor must fight his or her way on to the bus at a central bus station at which confusion seems always to reign. The confusion of the unwary visitor is matched by that of the locals, who jostle and shout in order to match buses with destinations and departure times. The buses themselves, though of varying vintages, are all lovingly cared for; the windscreen and the driver's area are decorated with small crosses, religious pictures, beads and other bric-a-brac. Like most country buses, they are almost invariably crowded with human travellers and, occasionally, other livestock. Large amounts of foodstuffs and other supplies are stowed under the bus or on the roof.

On the day we travelled to Topos our bus, which was on its way to the South Coast of Crete, was crowded as usual. Less commonplace was the (empty) coffin that accompanied us, tied to the roof. Our arrival with that coffin, while not altogether cheerful, did at least suggest that our short period of fieldwork in Topos would begin with an event of suitably anthropological interest. The flimsy construction of the coffin itself also foreshadowed the material circumstances of the people of Topos.

Topos itself is not an especially picturesque village. It is approached via a minor road that turns sharply uphill off the main north-south road. It is barely visible from the main road. Few of the tourists on their way to more popular coastal destinations are ever aware of the village's existence, unless they happen to find themselves on one of the slow buses, like ours, that call in there.

The bus drew into the village and stopped. It could not be called a square - just a place where two roads met and widened, and where the kafeneion was situated. We got off and retrieved our bags. The coffin was unloaded.

The driver got back in. The bus left. The villagers who had met the bus to retrieve goods for delivery left. We found ourselves standing alone. Nobody showed any great interest in us as we picked up our backpacks and transferred ourselves to the kafeneion. We had come to Topos in order to try to record some of the characteristic folk songs of this region in and around the White Mountains - *rhizitika tragoudhia.* ...

This account of our arrival at Topos on the island of Crete will be recognizable as an example of an 'arrival story' that may be found at or near the beginning of many published Mediterranean ethnographies. Indeed, it is reminiscent of typical ethnographic accounts from even further afield. As is common among such ethnographic introductions, it begins to construct a place that is 'elsewhere': it starts to demarcate the 'field' of the fieldwork. It constructs the ethnographer as an archetypal 'stranger'. It is also a characteristic shared with other accounts of this type - not least from Mediterranean ethnography - it promotes an image of the remote, isolated village, and plays up the vicissitudes that the ethnographer must endure in order to reach his or her desired goal. As I shall suggest in a later chapter, ethnographers are prone to represent themselves and their fieldwork in a quasi-heroic light, emphasising the remoteness, the strangeness of it all (and hence their perspicacity and perseverance in gaining their unique insight into their chosen setting.)

Parody, pastiche and intertextuality

As I have suggested, I think that the opening extract reproduced above is readily recognizable for what it is - a typical fragment of ethnographic writing. Indeed, the only potentially remarkable thing about that extract is that it is not reproduced from any published ethnography. I wrote it myself for the purpose of the lecture from which this essay is derived. In that sense, therefore, the extract is not authentic: not least insofar as it is not an 'extract' from anything, as the rest of that implied text does not exist. While not authentic, it is not fictional, however. Subject to the limits of recall, it is a perfectly reasonable account of real events. I and two other students from Cambridge did indeed arrive in Topos, a village in Crete, much in that fashion. We were indeed there with the express aim of recording folk-song, and I was there primarily to take the photographs. I was a student of anthropology and - ironically - one of my companions was Michael Herzfeld, now a Professor of Anthropology at Harvard and acknowledged as a leading (probably the leading) anthropologist of Modern Greece (e.g. Herzfeld 1985). Indeed, Herzfeld has reported on his own fieldwork on Crete (though not the student exercise we did together). In other words, my supposed ethnographic fragment is not quite authentic, but it is not pure fiction either. It is reconstructed from memory. It is also a parody. Insofar as it strikes a chord or rings a bell with fellow scholars, it is because it deliberately echoes and parallels other texts in the genre of Mediterranean Anthropology. My choice of Topos as the pseudonym for our village is, for instance, a recognizable device, directly recalling and parodying, say, Kenna's use of Nisos to name her small Aegean island (Kenna 1990). (*Topos* is simply the Greek word for 'place', just as *Nisos* is the Greek for 'island'.) Herzfeld likewise used words like Glendi to name Greek villages: a *glendi* is a party or celebration, such as a ceilidh. My choice is artful, therefore. It is doubly so, of course, in that topos is *also* the term used by Aristotle and rhetoricians to describe topics of argumentation. Topos is not merely a place, it is also - rhetorically speaking - a *commonplace*. Furthermore, of course, were I to continue my unwritten ethnography of song in the White Mountains, then perhaps Topos would be not only an argumentative commonplace, but might also become elevated to the function of Archetype. For in the construction of an ethnography (using that term to refer to the product of research, enshrined in the anthropological or sociological monograph) we regularly transform the local settings we study into the most general cateogries of social science.

However, to return to my earlier point: my fragment of text is a parody, and an act of memory. Now it is perfectly possible to construct and document an argument that runs: all ethnographic writing is a parodic act of remembering. Indeed, a strong version of that argument might be sustained to the effect that it is only possible for us to 'remember' - and so to reconstruct - a particular culture, place or people by virtue of our capacity to 'parody'. Our work may be thought of as parodic in two related senses. First, Michael Mulkay has proposed the view that all sociology - and by implication cognate disciplines too - are based on parody. Mulkay writes:

> ....I suggest that a parody is a secondary text which is closely based on (alongside of) an original text, but which differs from the original text in ways which reveal the true nature of the original text (it is central features) and at the same time the superiority of the secondary text....(Mulkay, 1985, p.238)

Here Mulkay is suggesting that the sociologist (or anthropologist - the disciplinary boundaries are not important) is dealing with primary or original texts, such as the transcripts of interviews with his or her hosts, or with other 'texts of the field', such as fieldnotes. From and with these texts the sociologist constructs *another* set of texts (papers, theses, monographs) that are - in this sense - parodies of the first. To that extent, then, one may speak of parody in this context - and it is a theme I shall return to.

Moreover, Mulkay notes briefly that the 'primary' texts drawn on for analysis may, for some scholars, be the texts written by other sociologists.

This brings me to my second set of connotations of 'parody'. For it would appear that we are able to produce our 'secondary' texts - our published ethnographies, for instance - insofar as we are able to parody other writing of a similar nature. I was able to produce my tiny fragment of the unwritten ethnography of Topos because there exist many such ethnographies that *have* been written, some of which I have read. My ethnography - for what it is worth - is recognizable because it is recognizably an example of a more general type of text. To put that into more obviously literary terms, its production and reception are possible because my text is understandable as part of a *genre*. It therefore has recognizable relations of intertextuality with other texts (not all of them other ethnographies). The analytic work we do, therefore, as fieldworkers, scholars and authors - whatever we call it, *verstehen*, interpretation, hermaneutic or whatever - is profoundly implicated with our competence and sensibilities as readers of texts. In other words, social worlds are describable and recognizable partly because we have textual models that have previously described other social worlds. My account of Topos would be possible by virtue of, say, Friedl's account of 'her' Greek village of Vasilika (Friedl (1962), Kenna's of Nisos (Kenna 1990), or Herzfeld's of Glendi (Herzfeld 1992). By that I do not mean that I or anyone else would simply copy them: parody is by no means the same as plagiarism.

The idea of parody and relations of intertextuality, of course, draw our attention to the fact that our ethnographies are far from unique. While each seeks to represent the particular, the local, it does so in a way that draws on the textual conventions of ethnography in general, and the conventions of particular genres. It is unwise to attempt a characterization of 'ethnography in general', indeed. For the various contrasting styles, traditions and genres of ethnographic writing provide powerful and pervasive frames of reference within which social worlds are reconstructed. There appear to be various dimensions of contrast between genres. There are, of course, differences between academic disciplines and national styles of scholarship. There are generational differences within particular traditions. In disciplines like anthropology and sociology there are also differences of genre that relate directly to the subject-matter and locale of the fieldwork itself. Among anthropologists, for instance, there are clear differences and continuities in the representation of particular regions, and in recent years a number of commentators have begun to sketch the interrelations of rhetoric and region (Fardon 1990; Atkinson 1992).

The characteristics of genre are, simultaneously, constraints and opportunities. Together, they create the possibility of the ethnographic enterprise. Genre constrains, in that it may furnish models and examples that limit how we think and how we write our ethnographies. For each genre is not innocent: each provides us with a perceptual and conceptual framework through which social reality is represented. The ethnographic genre - like a so-called paradigm - limits the ethnographic genre, in that it furnishes what Blumer described as directions along which to look. In a sense, then, an ethnographic genre suggests the cultural categories and grids that indicate what is thinkable and what is discoverable. It does not merely constrain what may be known *about* the field; it constrains what shall count *as* the field. More fundamentally and more powerfully - because tacitly - then the overt precepts of theory and methodology, the features of our ethnographic genres shape what shall be treated as worthy of description and susceptible to representation. It is, of course, a commonplace to note that even the most holistic of ethnographies is never quite that. All are selective, or selectively negligent. The implicit boundaries of what is included and what is excluded are inscribed in the genres.

Equally, of course, the conventions of genre create the very possibility of composition. What is discoverable in and of the field is also what is *writable*. Indeed, without the possibility of writing, it is doubtful whether there is a field, in the sense of anthropological or sociological fieldwork. We know, of course, that fields are not pre-given entities, and we know that they are not naturally bounded in time and space. They are not discovered, but *made* through a recurrent process of transactions. And yet, we can perhaps, go so far as to say that the field does not exist - that is, does not come into being - until we can write it into existence. The ethnographic genre is, therefore, the possibility of a discipline of social and cultural representation. It is, metaphorically, the *langue* that permits the *parole* of the individual ethnographer and the separate ethnography. These remarks are not intended to convey an extreme (and extremely silly) version of constructivism that suggests that reality may be conjured up out of nothingness by cognitive acts of individual actors. I am not proposing here that the ethnographer constructs the field of field research in that radical, and patently absurd, sense. There exist prior to the ethnographer's gaze the multitude of social practices and everyday activities that constitute mundane social existence. I am, however, suggesting that the objects of academic discourse we conventionally think of as 'fields' are consctructed partly through the practical transactions of the ethnographer, and partly by his or her textual practices in the construction of scholarly accounts.

In other words, the ethnography, with its generic, intertextual associations is an act of *collective* memory. The ethnographic text is constructed out of the shards of evidence that are the memorabilia of fieldwork, and the data are surveyed with the imagination of memory. Yet, for all that the ethnographic experience is a unique biographical episode or career, the memory that is brought to bear is not a private mental capacity. Rather, it is a collective memory, in part in the sense provided by Halbwachs (1992). Halbwachs, in his thoroughgoing Durkheimian fashion, argued that memories are *collective* representations. There is no need to appeal to a nebulous group mind in order to appreciate that even the personal experience of autobiographical memory is organized through socially shared resources. Culture and language give shape to *what* is memorable, and provide the framework for *how* it is to be remembered. Memory, then, is an act which is never independent of the social. The ethnography, likewise, is brought into the realm of shared knowledge through the devices of shared memory. The ethnographic genre is a collective device for the social construction of experiences recollected and reconstructed. It is necessary to realise, therefore, that the ethnographic account is not produced simply out of the data (whatever form the latter take). The various rhetorics of exploration, grounded theory and the like can, misleadingly, imply a thoroughly inductive approach. It is all too easy, even for the sophisticated commentator, to give the impression that analysis and composition proceed on the basis of a lone scholar struggling with the data with little or no interpretive frameworks to guide the enterprise. This owes a good deal to romantic imagery of the scholar or artist grappling with his or her chosen medium in a painful struggle to capture the inspiration of the moment. The ethnographic enterprise is not really like that (even though it may feel equally lonely and frustrating at times). The artistic endeavour is not of that kind either. The artist and the scholar are usually working in the knowledge of conventions and exemplars of other work, even when they consciously rebel against them. When the ethnographer seeks to represent aspects of the social world, his or her accounts are not spun out of thin air. We do not wrestle with our data with absolutely no ideas - implicit though they may be - of the kinds of products that are possible. Some of those models, examples and presuppositions are furnished by prior texts.

In these, and other, ways, therefore, the textual traditions of ethnographic work provide us with our parodic versions of social worlds. Indeed, we can perhaps go further, and suggest that we are dealing not only with parody, but with *pastiche* as well. If the parody is one particular form of self-conscious mimesis, then the pastiche is even more so. The pastiche produces a simulacrum - sometimes a grotesque likeness - out of the shreds and patches of an original model. Again, it is not a mere copy, for it is actively constructed. It is different from the original, but not original itself. The pastiche, then, is like that other variety of artifact beloved of anthropologists, the *bricolage*. Likewise, the ethnography is not merely a parody of the texts of the field. It is also a bricolage, not merely of sources or data, but of styles of representation too.

For our 'collective memory' is not a homogeneous tradition, any more than ours is a homogeneous culture. On the contrary, the ethnographic genre draws together the feature of many genres from within and beyond the confines of academic scholarship. There are intertextual relationships between individual ethnographies; there are also intertextual affinities and contrasts with a diverse range of non-ethnographic texts. For an unnecessarily large number of critics and commentators the affinities between ethnographic and other writing have constituted an offence. The textual models and similarities with fiction, journalism, biography and the like too readily seemed to undermine the credibility of ethnographic work. For those who mistook the shadow of science for its substance, the overtly literary character of a great deal of the ethnographic tradition detracted from its status in the domain of scholarly academic discourse. The taint of journalism, say, would be diagnosed by critics who endorsed a simple-minded set of distinctions - between fact and fiction, science and non-science, reality and representation.

In recent years, however, we have come to recognize that such discriminations are by no means simple: indeed, that they may even be spurious. Central to that intellectual change has been the renaissance of 'rhetoric'. Conceived in a broader sense perhaps than its classical counterparts, and drawing on more distinctively twentieth-century disciplines such as linguistics and semiotics, the 'rhetorical turn' in the human, social and indeed natural sciences has had far-reaching effects. It allows us to recognize the damaging consequences of the radical separation of science and rhetoric in the modern era and the emergence of what Snow (from a very different perspective) labelled 'the two cultures'. Those consequences were damaging not only for our collective understanding of the natural world and its representation, but for the humane disciplines as well.

Although it still creates ire and resentment in some quarters where views are entrenched, it is by no means novel or revolutionary to suggest that science is a human activity suffused with rhetoric. Distinguished contributions from North American, British and European authors have in recent years rapidly accumulated detailed accounts of the conventions that constitute the taken-for-granted representational devices that natural scientists have developed and deployed in order to construct and convey representations of natural order. One need only to allude to, say, Bazerman's sensitive and scholarly analysis of the experimental journal article as a genre in modern science (Bazerman 1988), or Myers' equally impressive work on the textual construction of biological knowledge (Myers 1990). Equally - and to extend the notion of 'rhetoric' to include various forms of representation - we are now aware of the many artful contrivances whereby diagrams, photographs, models, X-rays and the like rely on conventions of semiosis in scientific tests or presentations. The contributions of authors like Michael Lynch have played an important role in this context. We are now in a position to appreciate the character of such representational devices, in their cultural and historical context. Perhaps I may illustrate that point briefly with reference to my own current interests. Together with my colleagues Evelyn Parsons and Claire Batchelor, I am involved in a certain amount of ethnographic research on the scientific work of medical geneticists. Those scientists, in their laboratories and in their work with clinicians, produce and interpret an enormous array of representations, of course. Their technical competence resides not only in the techniques (the embodied knowledge) needed to produce those texts and representations; it also rests on their capacity to read and to use them for theoretical and practical purposes.

The particular artifact used by geneticists, and shared among the clinical scientists and the clinical practitioners, is the pedigree. That is, the formal, conventional representation of biological relationships of consanguinity, used to plot the intergenerational transmission of genetic material. They are also used to identify the patterns of inheritance among members of a particular 'family'. Such representations are massively familiar, and cognate artifacts are well known elsewhere - not least, of course, the 'family tree', and the kinship diagram that is part of the stock-in-trade of social anthropologists. It is so familiar that we are often in danger of overlooking its character as an artifact and a convention of representation: not least because of the congruence between what we take to be the 'natural' facts of molecular biologic and sexual reproduction on the one hand, and the cultural arrangements of Anglo-American kinship on the other. The 'pedigree' unites and naturalizes biology and kinship in a metaphorical representation. (That metaphor has its own connotations and cultural history too: including the family-trees of the nobility; the breeding records of animal husbandry and the blood-lines of thoroughbred horses; the everyday genealogies of the family bible; the genealogical charters of clans and lineages; the legal requirements of testamentary disposition; and so on. Even the pedigree has intertextual affinities).

The general programme of the 'rhetoric of inquiry' as it has come to be called is by no means confined to the natural sciences. On the contrary, the rhetorical turn has been pursued and explored across a wide diversity of humanities and social sciences. If the natural sciences are rhetorical, the latter are equally so: history; philosophy; economics; anthropology; sociology; psychology. To return to my earlier remarks - the intertextual possibilities of parody and pastiche in the ethnography are possible by virtue of the 'literary' or 'rhetorical' resources that we draw on in the construction of sociological or anthropological accounts. Indeed, it is the recognition of our *textual construction of reality* that gives rise to some of the most lively and challenging reflections about and on behalf of ethnography today.

A recognition of the conventional quality and the literary and rhetorical antecedents of the ethnographic text raises questions about the distinctive characteristics of ethnography as a genre or textual product. It is not enough - in the eyes of many commentators - simply to acknowledge that our texts are conventionally ordered; nor indeed that they are, in the broadest sense 'fictitious'. It is important to recognize that textual devices serve not merely aesthetic interests, but also have inescapable ethical implications. A good deal of anthropological reflection has focused on the textual representation (or repression) of the Author and the Other. Here anthropologists and sociologists find common interests with more general cultural critics, such as Said or Spivak (Coffey and Atkinson 1995).

It is argued in this context that a paradox lies at the heart of the ethnographic endeavour and 'the ethnography' as a textual product. On the one hand is the ethnographer's personal and epistemology commitment to engagement and participation - to 'participant observation' in its fullest sense. The epistemology of participant observation rests on the principle of interaction and intersubjectivity, and on the 'reciprocity of perspectives' between social actors. The classic texts of ethnographic reportage, on the other hand, have - it is often claimed - too often inscribed a radical distinction between the Ethnographer/Author and the Other. The 'realist' techniques of standard ethnographic writing may thus endow the ethnographer with a privileged gaze that reproduces the authorial omniscience characteristic of much realist fiction and other 'authoritative' written styles. The 'traditional' ethnographic text, it is claimed, brings actors and culture together under the auspices of a simple, all-encompassing point of view. By contrast, the 'Other' is rendered solely as the object of the ethnographer's gaze. The 'voice' of the Ethnographer is privileged, that of the Other is muted.

As a consequence, there have been various attempts to produce ethnographic texts that replace the'monologic' mode with 'dialogic' forms, in which the text allows for a multiplicity of 'voices'. This perspective is intended to bring together textual, methodological and ethical commitments. Unfortunately, at the present time, the call for 'dialogic' forms of representation results in disappointing outcomes. It is not enough merely to 'let the actors speak for themselves', nor yet to reproduce transcripts of interviews and interrogations. Indeed, the contemporary fashion for 'dialogic' ethnography (or rather, the fashion for appeals for it) seems all too often an apology for a rather anaemic variety of cultural pluralism: that is, a 'relativism' of the weakest sort (see Atkinson 1992).

In a similar, critical vein have been the advocates of feminist points of view. The textual practices of privileged 'Western' observers may be compared with the inscription of a privileged masculine discourse. There have, therefore, been a number of attempts to produce feminist texts that subvert the taken-for-granted formats. Krieger's 'stream of consciousness' style may be cited as one such exemplar (Krieger 1983). The feminist appraisal of ethnographic writing is in turn part of a more general re-evaluation of social-scientific writing from a feminist perspective, and a renewed interest in various genres - most notably biography and autobiography. Authors such as Smith (1987), or Stanley and Wise (1983), provide a powerful and coherent link between a feminist standpoint and a readiness to treat textual focus as problematic. That concern is epistemological and ethical, personal and professional. Form a feminist standpoint, of course, these are all implicative of one another.

Behind and beyond these critiques, commentaries and experiments lies the (often incoherent) appeal of 'postmodernism'. The 'postmodern' is reflected in the rhetorical arrangements of 'the ethnography' as text. The postmodern ethnography may thus explore (but not seek to reconcile) the discontinuities, paradoxes and inconsistencies of culture and action. From a postmodernist perspective, the 'classic' ethnography - 'modern- in inspiration - brought the various fragmentary representations of social life under the ordering of superordinate narratives.

The postmodernist perspective proposes a radical appraisal of ethnography and the ethnographic text. Tyler, for instance, rejects any claim that ethnography can be said to 'represent' anything in the social world. He prefers the terminology of 'evoking' rather than representing. He claims that the rhetoric of evocation 'frees ethnography from mimesis and the inappropriate mode of scientific rhetoric that entails "objects", "facts", "descriptions", "inductions", "generalizations", "verification", "experiment", "truth", and like concepts that, except as empty invocations, have no parallels either in the experience of ethnographic fieldwork or in the writing of ethnographies' (Tyler 1986: 130)

Now there are issues of real substance in the postmodernist critique, and in the feminist perspective, as in the more general turn to the rhetoric of inquiry. Nevertheless, there is a danger. In recent years there has been such a consistent emphasis on the rhetoric, and on the poetics of ethnography, that there has been some danger of undue attention being paid to 'literary' and 'aesthetic' issues. Problems of logic and inference have been obscured. Recognition that scholarly texts have conventional and literary aspects seems to have led some commentators and practitioners to extremes. Textual experimentation - sometimes to the point of obscurantism - has now been undertaken in the name of 'postmodernism', for instance, in the wake of a fashion for postmodern science have come several self-proclaimed postmodern ethnographies. They have, in various ways, experimented with textual forms and styles that disrupt and fragment the surfaces of the classic realist text. Some - in characteristically postmodern fashion - deploy a variety of styles, including pastiche of non-realist literary forms.

In one sense, it is difficult not to applaud the overt experimentation with literary representation. We recognize that no literary style is a 'natural' mode of representation; none is a neutral medium. Equally, we recognize that there is an arbitrary element in any and every set of literary or rhetorical conventions. On the other hand, two reservations are in order. First, partly aesthetic, is the realization that contemporary experimentation with modes of writing (whether or not explicitly postmodernist or feminist) are mostly uninspiring. They have a certain intrinsic interest by virtue of their status and 'unconventional' sociological or anthropological texts. But they fall far short of the literary models of even the most pale approximations to the literary achievements of *modernism* (never mind postmodernism!) Krieger's 'stream-of-consciousness' is nothing of the sort when set against major modernist authors. There is nothing in the writing of the social sciences to rival the precision, detail and complexity of, say, 'The Wandering Rocks' episode in Joyce's *Ulysses* (which episode, we are told, Joyce planned with a map of Dublin and a stop-watch in order to capture the dense interweaving of actions and interactions in time and space). There is little or nothing that actually inscribes alternating voices in the social sciences that comes close to, say, Faulkner's *The Sound and the Fury*. There seems nothing that even compares with a Dos Passos on modern American living. In one sense, therefore, there may have been a failure of nerve. The production of ethnographic texts has certainly not kept pace with the radical critique of ethnographic writing. Indeed, in this context it is worth noting that the contemporary advocates of 'alternative literary forms' in the sociology of scientific knowledge in question draw on extremely well-worn literary models; their only novelty or strangeness lies in the fact that, say, a one-act play is being used to reconstruct a sociological or scientific dispute. The playlet itself is likely to be quite lacking in any innovation or experimentation in itself.

This is not an appeal for an unfettered and undisciplined approach to writing ethnography. There is nothing to be gained from an undisciplined appeal to the *avant garde*. We do not need experimentation just for the sake of it. A recognition of our own literary conventions is not merely license to test and transgress those conventions' boundaries; it is also a *mandate* to use writing in a disciplined and principled way. (To borrow a distinction from the sociology of work and occupations). To write as I did at the beginning of 'parody' and 'pastiche' is, perhaps, to convey too readily a sense of flippant detachment. But that would be wrong: as wrong as the false dichotomy between science and rhetoric. Scholarship and rhetoric imply choices, decisions and responsibility. They both imply both aesthetic and ethical judgments. A self-conscious awareness of the *forms* of our inquiry implies a *responsibility* for those forms. While conventional - and hence arbitrary - modes of representation are, for that very reason, implicative of how we can understand social worlds, and how that understanding is constructed and shared. We may use conventions for sound purposes, we may confront and transgress them for good reasons, we may juxtapose them and mingle different genres for deliberate effect. We are not, however, entitled to do so irresponsibly.

Furthermore, the 'poetics' of our own written productions must surely alert us to the poetics of everyday life. When we construct *our* parodies, we are constructing them partly out of the texts and performances of the social world we reconstruct. Consequently, contemporary ethnography must adopt a disciplined and principled relationship between *its* poetics and the *ethnopoetics* of the life-world. We need to pay even more systematic attention to the tropes and narratives of everyday experience; to the spoken performances that enact the mundane and the routine; to the ceremonial forms of interaction ritual. Schutz suggested that the work of the phenomenological sociologist is couched in 'second-order' constructs that must be derived from, and must have affinity with, the 'first-order' constructs of 'the man or woman in the street'. In much the same way, the second-order 'poetics' of our texts must still reflect the rhetoric and practices of those whose lives we reconstruct.

Whether or not we need to be 'redesigning ethnography' I am not sure. I am, however, convinced of two things. First, ethnography has been and is continually redesigned. As a collection of texts, as a genre or genres, it has changed repeatedly throughout this century, and it will continue to do so. Secondly, I am convinced that 'redesigning' is the work of Ethnography itself. We identify the 'design' in spoken and enacted culture, in the recurrent patterns and routines of action, and we redesign them as we craft our representations and recollections. In recent years it has become commonplace to identify a 'crisis of representation' in the cultural and human disciplines. It is not at all necessary to think in terms of 'crisis' - unless it be in that word's original sense of a 'turning-point'. For a growing self-awareness of the rhetoric of inquiry provides one powerful way of reasserting the essential unity of the scholarly disciplines. Not, that is, through the sterile impositions of a unified method, in the fashion of the logical positivists in the search for a unified science, but in the recognition of the human work of understanding, interpretation and representation that is common to us all. The rhetoric of inquiry and the poetics of everyday life together suggest a mode of inquiry that is grounded in a humanistic concern with the responsibilities of representation.

4   Supervising the text

Introduction

This essay is concerned primarily with the education of ethnographers themselves. As qualitative research methods are taken up by increasing numbers of researchers, so the supervision of ethnographic work becomes a professional responsibility for more academics. In Britain, recent policies and debates concerning the quality and nature of the Ph.D. in social sciences have led us to focus our minds on the processes and outcomes of Ph.D. supervision (For recent documentation of that debate, see Burgess 1994.) Much of that heart-searching stems from institutional pressures over Ph.D. completion rates and the average length of time taken to finish the doctorate. They have, however, prompted more wide-spread reflection on the content and conduct of advanced research training. This paper has its origins in reflection of that sort.   The significance of the Ph.D. in the social and educational sciences goes well beyond the specific policy concerns concerning numbers and completion rates, however. Most social scientists -- ethnographers in particular -- learn research skills and orientations of lifelong importance during their doctoral research. The relative autonomy and time available to the postgraduate student are luxuries denied to teaching academics for most of their careers. The Ph.D. thesis may lay the foundations for a subsequent career as a scholar. Many of the important ethnographic monographs in Britain, North America and elsewhere have their origins in Ph.D. theses. Over and above the methodological precepts available in textbooks and courses, much of the craft wisdom and the oral tradition of interpretative research is transmitted from generation to generation through the supervisory relationship. It is therefore important that the supervision of postgraduate research should be subject to critical reflection. The direction - as well as the conduct - of qualitative research is multi-faceted. It calls for a range of different skills, and draws on experience of diverse academic activities. This chapter will consider the the supervisor's role and the work of the student in relation to styles of writing. There are, of course, many styles of qualitative research in the social sciences, and there is no attempt here to cover them all. Rather, attention will be restricted to ethnographic fieldwork of a fairly traditional sort.

The student and supervisor of the ethnography together face a potentially daunting task. The classic ethnography is a text of some complexity and considerable scope. Would-be doctoral candidates who pursue ethnographic research may find themselves triply burdened: time-consuming and often unpredictable fieldwork is followed by complex and labour-intensive analysis, which in turn is followed by major tasks of writing. The construction of 'an ethnography' calls for considerable organizational and creative effort and the ethnographer can rarely fall back on the more ritualised formats that are available for some genres of scientific reporting.

All of those who have supervised ethnographic research, as well as those who have undertaken it, know how important an element the *writing* is. This is so for a number of reasons, both practical and methodological. Not least is the sheer enormity of the task. There is, of course, no inherent or necessary relationship between a style of research method and the absolute length of text which reports that research. Nevertheless, there is a conventional and traditional relationship at work. The discursive nature of qualitative research and its reporting leads readily to the production of long and complex texts. Even where universities impose word limits on dissertations, we commonly find ethnographic theses stretching and over-running those limits. Where there is no such external constraint, then the two-volume ethnography is a type as recognizable as the nineteenth century triple-decker novel. Many of the available role models incline us towards length. The classic ethnographic monograph in social anthropology, sociology or education is usually a substantial piece of writing. In the case of my own doctoral work (Atkinson 1976), an obvious model was *Boys in White* (Becker *et al.*, 1961), which runs to over 400 pages. Admittedly, that was written by a research team of four, but tomes of similar length - indeed a series of volumes spanning a lifetime's scholarly output - can confront the novice. The point here is not that *Boys in White* is 'too long'. There is obviously no ideal or 'correct' length for every or any ethnography. Rather, the ethnographic genre inclines novices and their supervisors towards texts of unmanageable proportions. This is but one obvious way in which the discursive reconstruction of social worlds is a major task.

Any commitment to a notion of holism is likely to lead the researcher towards lengthy writing tasks. He or she may feel impelled to produce long descriptive accounts of a wide range of actors, settings and actions. Often in the absence of more summary measures and indices the author of the ethnography may feel it necessary to try to persuade the reader by sheer volume of examples, breadth and depth of coverage, length of exposition and so on. Whereas for some student authors, the weight of numbers provides intellectual and existential security, for the author of a qualitative study the volume of text may fulfill a similar function. In any event, the 'weight' of evidence, the burden of proof as it were, is frequently carried by the density and complexity, as well as the sheer bulk of the writing. The burden of proof thus becomes an intellectual burden for the would-be author, as well as a major practical task. The writing of the ethnography is, for many students and practitioners, the most demanding task of composition ever faced in the course of a career.

Length, then, is one far from trivial reason why the writing of the thesis (and indeed published monograph) may occupy a disproportinately significant place in the overall enterprise. Certainly, the character of qualitative research means that the normal usage and connotations of 'writing up' are inappropriate. The conventional models of the research process which imply clearly demarcated phases (e.g. design, data collection, analysis) and treat the 'writing up' not only as a separate, but relatively straightforward phase, do not fit. The 'writing up' of qualitative research is a much more extensive and pervasive feature of the research process. The important issues of ethnographic text go far beyond the issue of length per se: I use it by way of introduction to more far-reaching issues of ethnographic scholarship. As scholars are increasingly led to recognise, the very essence of the ethnographic enterprise requires us to pay close attention to the process of writing.

The textual reconstruction of reality

Data collection itself is often a 'literary' activity - especially if it involves the construction of fieldnotes. It is self-evident that fieldnotes are mediated and contrived representations of social events. When the ethnographer produces lengthy 'processed' notes, he or she unavoidably uses basic literary or rhetorical devices to produce realistic and vivid accounts of observed settings and actions. An account of every conceivable detail, minute by minute, is practically impossible. It would also violate our normal expectations concerning the writing and reading of intelligible accounts. The author of fieldnotes therefore constructs narrative accounts of social action, and uses metaphorical usage to produce descriptions and characterizations. Many ethnographers have cited extracts from their fieldnotes by way of illustration or as evidence in their published products. It is clear that many scholars construct fairly polished, worked-up accounts that draw on a full range of conventions of realist narratives. We glimpse these texts in their fragmentary appearances in papers and monographs. They are rarely available *in toto* for critical inspection. There are some methodological precepts available in the relevant textbooks on how to record one's experiences and impressions in systematic fashion. But we have precious little collective understanding of the literary conventions that are used, or of the traditions and genres that may have evolved. The construction of these 'primary' texts remains under-explored. In the absence of standard public availability of fieldnotes and journals, there is no systematic analysis of fieldnotes as text. Equally, therefore, there is a dearth of even conventional wisdom among experienced practitioners concerning the construction and interpretation of those accounts. There is a very clear parallel between the heroic imagery of the 'lone ethnographer' writing his or her notes, keeping up the daily ration of observation and reporting, and the lone author, wrestling with a recalcitrant medium and an elusive inspiration (cf. Brodkey 1987). But, as Brodkey reminds us, writing is a social act, and when it is also a *sociological* act, then it behoves us to take explicit account of its accomplishment. There is need for more than trial-and-error on the part of the apprentice, or rule-of-thumb advice on the part of the supervisor. If the database of an ethnography is to include the 'literary' construction of fieldnotes, then there is need for explicit and critical awareness of what conventional resources are being brought to bear. Collectively, we need secondary analysis of the poetics of fieldnotes. There is a lack of critical vocabulary with which the oral tradition and its craft knowledge can be brought under critical scrutiny. A framework for critical understanding is required if elementary aspects of the ethnographic task are to be transmitted and supervised in a disciplined fashion. Much of the necessary groundwork remains to be done. It calls for an acquaintance with contemporary scholarship in cultural and critical theory. The same is true when it comes to the work of constructing and interpreting the final 'products' of ethnography -- dissertations, monographs and papers.

The analysis of the data is dependent on their arrangement and discussion in extended discursive presentations. Quite apart from niceties of theory and epistemology, it is a practical task of some magnitutude. It is intellectually demanding and time-consuming. The successful construction of an ethnographic account may involve repeated drafting and re-drafting of working papers and draft chapters before the ordering and presentation of the material starts to 'work'. There is, moreover, a strong element of unpredictability in these tasks. As author or as supervisor one is often unsure as to how the 'analysis' will work out, what connections are to be found and elaborated on, until preliminary drafting has been done. The analytic induction of categories, themes and relationships, the explication of meaning and the understanding of action may all proceed via the writing itself. Neither the novice nor the experienced practitioner can assume that 'the findings' will be formulated as a set of propositions, simply to be reported and filled in through a more-or-less mechanical set of compositional steps. The role of the supervisor may need to be more actively focused on the writing than is the case in other styles of research. The supervisor will need to be concerned not simply with the progress of the writing and keeping the student on schedule; the interest will go beyond the factual accuracy of the reportage; rather, the supervisor may need to consider the *form* of the writing. A systematic understanding of the work, to be shared between supervisor and apprentice, will encompass an appreciation of the textual possibilities and choices that are available, the characteristics of exemplary texts, the use of narrative, metaphor, and other tropes.

There is, therefore, a profound sense in which the writing is an integral feature of the research enterprise. It is not always appreciated by colleagues unversed in qualitative research, but the anthropological or sociological 'findings' are inscribed in the ways we write about things: they are not detached from the presentation of observations, reflections and interpretations. We all know how difficult we can find it, on our own or our students' behalf, to answer 'What are your conclusions?' or 'What have you proved?' It is possible to derive propositional theory and summary findings from ethnographic research and equivalent writing. But it is normally a very pale reflection of the 'thick' descriptive work of the thesis or monograph, and in no way substitutes for it. The desired response to the naive question is 'Well, read the ethnography'.

A pertinent case in point, although perhaps an extreme version of the 'literary' style, is the published work of Erving Goffman. Lofland (1980) demonstrates the point with reference to several of Goffman's texts. From *Asylums* - the nearest Goffman got to a standard ethnographic monograph - one can derive propositions of the order of:

> *If* persons are placed in total institutions, *then* their selves will be mortified.

> *If* persons are placed in total institutions, *then* they will develop secondary adjustments to protect themselves from the identity implications of the organization's theory of human nature.

But propositions of this sort seem exceptionally jejune in comparison with the dense complexity of Goffman's own texts. Indeed, Goffman's sociological analysis is substantially conveyed through the rhetorical devices and formats of his published works, and some features of his distinctive approach to composition will be explored in another chapter.

The 'writing up' of the qualitative study is not merely a major and lengthy task, it is *intrinsic* to the analysis, the theory and the findings. The success or failure of the entire project can depend on the felicity of the writing. To a considerable extent, therefore, the craft of qualitative research implies craft skill in organizing the products of that research into satisfying and plausible products. On the whole, however, students and their advisers have little methodological advice to guide them in the construction of ethnographic texts. The majority of methods textbooks are reticent - if not totally silent - on the topic of writing. That is understandable enough, given the paucity of shared knowledge about the processes and products involved. We have devoted a great deal of methodological imagination to fieldwork practicalities, ethics, social relationships, data storage and retrieval, even theory building - but, until very recently, much less to writing. To a considerable extent methods texts in qualitative traditions, despite authors' intentions to the contrary, have reflected the implicit logic of more positivistic styles. The collection of valid and reliable data is treated as paramount. Their literary transformation into texts is relegated to the extra-curricular. Some general methods texts do include advice on writing, but they tend to lack grounding in a technical appreciation of critical theory.

I suppose that we have all been aware, if only at a preconscious level, that successful ethnographies have certain kinds of stylistic, aesthetic qualities. We ourselves have often assimilated the stylistic characteristics of admired exemplars. Lacking clear guidelines, even of a typological sort, we have perhaps advised a student to take an admired monograph from the bookshelf and emulate it. It is noteworthy that this strategy would no longer pass for sound methodological advice for any other phase or feature of the research. The collective amnesia concerning literary modes of representation reflects a number of historical contrasts and oppositions. Modern scientific discourse has diverged from its erstwhile companion of Rhetoric. Until very recent years rhetoric has been neglected (except for a very enfeebled existence in the teaching of composition to American undergraduates). Rhetoric has been relegated to mere presentation and 'rhetoric' contrasts with matters of substance. In a broader vein, the crudest images that have governed our conceptions of positive science have been dismissive of the aesthetic elements of scholarly endeavour. More specifically, the search for academic respectability and the supposed claims for well-founded 'factual' status have easily led qualitative scholarship to distance itself from more overtly literary activities. The indication of close affinities and stylistic similarities between ethnography and journalism or fictional writing is sometimes treated as a threat to our scholarly standards and the veracity of our accounts.

In recent years, however, a small but growing number of anthropologists, sociologists and others in the 'human sciences' have turned their attention to the textual character of our productions (Brown, 1977, 1983; Clifford, 1978, 1981, 1983; Crapanzano, 1977; Geertz, 1983, 1988; Marcus, 1980; Marcus and Cushman, 1982; Van Maanen, 1988.) The specific analytic approaches vary, and include the range of perspectives current in literary- critical theory. The various authors also espouse different epistemological and political positions. Analyses have included attempts to explicate ideological inscriptions in textual practices; the uses of literary tropes to convey sociological or anthropological insight; textual devices to establish the authority of the author; varieties of narrative and genre to be found among ethnographic texts. While approaches differ in their emphases, they are in broad agreement in suspending the conventional distinction between 'fact' and 'fiction', in the recognition that *all* texts are constructed in accordance with socially shared conventions. The authors and the readers of 'factual' accounts draw on conventions actively to 'make sense', just as do the readers and writers of 'fiction'. This perspective does not result in a promiscuous or nihilistic approach. The methodological suspension of taken-for-granted distinctions allows for the recognition and exploration of the textuality of 'factual' accounts; it does not lead to a disregard for the circumstances of their production.

Irrespective of the epistemological or methodological claims for a piece of research, the text in which it is reported must be *persuasive*. This is the guiding rationale for Edmondson's application of rhetorical analyses to a sample of sociological texts (Edmondson 1984). Edmondson's analytic scope is modest, and the emphasis on classical rhetoric means that a much broader tradition of critical theory is glossed over. Nevertheless, Edmondson's treatment is useful: it provides a clear exposition of various textual devices whereby sociological authors persuade (or attempt to persuade) their readers of the cogency and strength of their argument and of their evidence. The examples chosen to illustrate qualitative research methods are Rex and Moore's *Race, Community and Conflict* and Willis's *Learning to Labour*. Edmondson addresses a number of related issues. First, attention is drawn to the achievement of *ordering* and *relative emphasis* in the chosen texts. Of Willis, for instance, it is noted that his book has a rather unusual structure:

> The book is explicitly divided into two sections. The first presents a graphic, descriptive 'ethnography'; the second contains a detailed and heavily theorised 'analysis'. Edmondson suggests that this particular arrangement enables the reader to evolve a certain personal response to its subjects *before* the author advances a detailed sociological account of their situation. The response which the first part of the book is clearly intended to evoke is one of sympathy; sympathy not just in the sense of particular feelings towards Willis's subjects, but also in the sense of a preparedness to consider their points of view and to refrain from the dismissive evaluations of their conduct which are usual (the book makes clear) from people outside their own class and group. (p.42)

It is noteworthy that Willis presents the more engaging aspects of 'the lads' in the earlier passages, while the discussions of their 'sexism' and 'racism' are kept back: 'they are arranged, that is, in order of least likelihood to alienate the reader' (p.44).

Secondly, Edmondson draws attention to the use of 'examples' - and deals especially with the chosen texts' use of atypical and unrepresentative examples or illustrations. In that context Edmondson emphasizes that the *reader* is often required to draw conclusions and see contrasts. The analysis of Willis and Rex and Moore underlines the fact that the ethnography communicates by way of a persuasive relationship with the reader, rather than through formal models. Writing, for instance, of the use of quotations in *Learning to Labour*, Edmondson suggests

...we should not regard quotations such as those from Joey and

> Councillor Collett in the light of evidence as it is used in the natural sciences, and that the question whether they are literally typical in the statistical sense does not arise.... If instead we regard such citations as rhetorical devices for enabling and encouraging readers to perceive the force of general remarks, we can expect examples to exhibit particularly concentrated cases of what happens generally but, perhaps, less remarkably. (p.50)

Edmondson goes on to suggest that 'Forceful examples compensate the reader for his or her narrower experience of the field than the author's....' (ibid.)

As Edmondson demonstrates, the use of examples is important - functioning as they do as 'actual types':

> These examples, I believe, function rhetorically as signs: signs as symptoms of states in some way which enables the reader to interpret future situations, and only very rarely necessary signs of states of affairs. (p.52)

Edmondson's analysis alerts us to the pervasive feature of ethnographic texts: the interweaving of extracts, episodes and narratives on the one hand, and interpretation, observation, commentary and generalization on the other.

Edmondson's rhetorical analysis does not tell us anything we do not practice already, and it is a disappointingly sparse treatment of the potential range of topics. Nevertheless, we are usefully alerted to the fact that our, and our students', written products very largely stand or fall on the successful manipulation of rhetorical or literary conventions. The ethnographic thesis and monograph are members of a genre, and are expcted to correspond to the canons of that genre. Or, more precisely, we should recognize that there have been and are several sub-types of ethnographic genre, each with its own set of transformations on the basic conventional requirements.

John Lofland's is one of the few discussions by an experienced reader and writer of ethnographic work in sociology of how such conventions inform the reception of such texts (Lofland 1980). His observations derive from editorial work on journal submissions. Many of the general points are, however, common to article-length and thesis or monograph-length texts. Lofland's contribution is based on an analysis of referees' comments on papers reporting qualitative research, and his general expertise in the area. While it is clear that his remarks bear on more than just this issue, it is clear that content and style are inextricably intertwined in readers' receptions and reports. The reader of qualitative research cannot proceed 'as if' there were a neutral textual format independent of the scientific message to be conveyed. Lofland himself comments on this, noting that there is a division within sociology when it comnes to styles of reporting:

At one extreme, practitioners of laboratory and experimental work share a highly routinized set of working procedures and schemes for reporting research. Drawing from physical science models of inquiry perhaps facilitates their achieving such consensus. The stylistic and organizational features of their publications reproduce the stylistic and organizational features of physical science journals in particularly striking fashion. While not nearly as shared and codified, demographic and survey practitioners still draw upon a rather consensual pool of research strategies, technical steps, and standardized conceptions of the structure and content of their research reports. Moreover, one even senses a high degree of working agreement among library researchers who employ bodies of historical and substantive materials. (p.101)

In contrast, Lofland suggests a relative lack of consensus among those who report qualitative research findings:

...qualitative field research seems distinct in the degree to which its practitioners lack a public, shared, and codified conception of how what they do is done, and how what they report should be formulated. (p.101)

Of course, as Lofland himself acknowledges, the uniformity of the more clearly 'positivist' styles is itself a textual achievement - a matter of organization and style. Indeed, one strand of contemporary sociology of science pays particular attention to the literary representation of scientific findings and discoveries. On the other hand, though Lofland is correct in suggesting a lack of consensual models for the reporting of qualitative research, that does not imply a total lack of available models and devices. On the contrary, there are many generic conventions that inform the production of the text and its reading. Lofland goes on to discuss several evaluative criteria that are applied to qualitative research reports, each of which implies some textual element or arrangement.

First, there is the criterion invoked by readers which reflects the extent to which 'The report was organized by means of a *generic* conceptual framework.' (p.102). This refers to the extent to which a particular topic or setting is 'framed' according to more general themes. Such themes are used not simply as explicit sociological theory, but as more general articulatory themes, images and devices. The successful text weaves together the local and the generic - often by means of metaphorical allusions - in achieving a satisfying mixture of data and discussion, example and generalization. Interestingly, Lofland suggests that readers can predict the presence of a generic frame of reference from the opening sentences of a report. He cites the opening of Bigus (1972) as an instance of the successful deployment of such an introductory framing passage:

> America is a service society - so much so that essentially non-service institutions, such as stores, take on service-like characteristics.... This emphasis on service has given rise to a prepnderance of a particular kind of social activity, which I shall refer to as 'cultivating', and to an associated kind of social relationship which I will refer to as a 'cultivated relationship'.

This passage is used to frame an ethnographic account of the daily relationship between milkmen and their customers. The sort of 'framework' is detected by the reader at the outset, and provides him or her with an initial attitude, from which the significance of the paper is foreshadowed and projected. While openings like the Bigus passage state their theme they have the rhetorical function of persuading the sympathetic reader that the report addresses 'real' or 'important' themes *and* that the specific case to be explored is a relevant one.

Lofland goes on to suggest that readers who positively evaluate a 'generic' frame will find unsatisfactory reports that do no use organizational motifs of that sort. He refers, among others, to the 'Then They Do This' style, in which a report is organized so that it 'makes evident that participants do many kinds of things over and over, hour to hour, day to day, week to week'. Interestingly, Lofland notes that a text can - as it were - 'get away with' such an organizational format provided that the setting is sufficiently 'exotic': otherwise readers will allege that the text is merely based on 'cute', 'interesting', or 'startling' descriptive content.

Lofland goes on to detail other types of evaluative criteria invoked by readers of research reports. Readers may seek a 'novel frame'; or, when absolute freshness is impossible, then at least a 'slightly late' frame may be employed - that is, somebody else's recent novelty. As Lofland says:

> In recent years, the frames of Erving Goffman have been applied with particular assiduousness. Researchers report: yes, mental hospitals are total institutions; yes, this or that category of deviant experiences stigma; yes, inmates do use 'making out' devices. Slightly more novel, look over here, public housing has characteristics of total institutions. (pp. 105-6)

Readers, Lofland reports, find such second-hand novelties acceptable up to a point, but beyond that point the 'frame starts to lose its novelty value, and the readers are likely to condemn the text as mere dreary repetition'. The achievement of adequate novelty and freshness is not simply a function of which authors and examples are selected in order to illuminate the findings. To a considerable extent, the 'freshness' of the presentation will depend upon the literary skills with which those allusions, connotations, examples and citations are deployed. The reader will be swayed by criteria which are partly aesthetic: the 'lightness of touch' whereby other authors, studies and empirical parallels are filled in and elaborated on; the appositeness of those comparisons and contrasts; the extent to which they reveal 'imagination' and depart from the obvious and hackneyed.

The extreme example of the latter failing is contained in Lofland's type of the 'intro text style':

> ...notions that are 'common knowledge' in American society or that sociologists can find in elementary textbooks will likely be defined as 'obvious'. Few qualitative field reports discover such introductory textbook frames as socialization, norms, deviance, social control, culture or informal organization. (p.106)

The successful text, it would appear, is neither so 'novel' as to be outre and bizarre, nor so familar as to be stale. Moreover, as Lofland indicates, a successful textual arrangement should be adequately elaborated and enriched. First, the analytic 'frame' should be 'elaborated' - it should be couched in a text which 'specifies constituent elements of the frame, draws out implications, shows major variations, and uses all these as the means by which the qualitative data are organized and presented'. Further, for many readers, it should be 'eventful' - richly endowed with 'concrete interactional events, incidents, occurrences, episodes, anecdotes, scenes and happenings someplace in the real world'. On the other hand, it should not be over-burdened with the repetitious rehearsal of incidents and illustrations. Otherwise, it may topple over into the failing of being 'hyper-eventful'. These delicate balances are achieved in the texture of the writing itself.

A final evaluative criterion is closely related: the analytic frame and the qualitative data it comments on should be 'interpenetrated' if the text is to be judged satisfactory:

> ... taken separately, each is likely to be viewed as having little sociological interest or merit.... The frame taken separately is dull because the reader has little conception of the concrete empirical reality to which the frame might refer. The 'data' alone are dull because the reader has no notion of what sort of social structure or process might be involved. But interpenetrated through minute and continual alternation between data and frame-elements the whole is more than the parts. (pp. 108-9)

These by no means exhaust Lofland's observations, and his are not exhaustive of the textual arrangements of qualitative sociology. They are not alluded to in order to produce a prescriptive model for ethnographic texts, but to illustrate the sort of thing that sociological readers (including, presumably, supervisors and external examiners) seem to bring to such texts in evaluating their success or failure. The most important general issue to emerge from Lofland's analysis, as from Edmondson's, is the importance of textual arrangement itself. The text has a certain force or effect which is not based simply on some evaluation of whether it is 'correct' or not. Indeed, it is difficult to think how *any* written or spoken text could convey 'facts' or 'findings', let alone analyses, hypotheses, conjectures, criticisms and refutations without recourse to conventionally appropriate textual formats. In the reader's evaluative readings, then, form and content are inextricably linked. The text need not simply transcribe or report, but it must also persuade. The reader must be drawn into its own frame of reference, and come to share the perspectives of the text; it must be found plausible and engaging, arresting or novel; it must establish relations of identity and difference with other equivalent texts; it must establish relations of similarity and difference with the social world it reports - it needs to reproduce a recognizable world of concrete detail, but not appear to be an unremarkable recapitulation of it.

Lofland's analysis is important, in that it highlights - from actual experience - the bases of readers' judgments. It does little, however, to illuminate the fine detail of how 'literary' and 'rhetorical' conventions are used to construct plausible texts. Among recent sociological commentators Van Maanen (1988) is notable for his contribution on ethnographic writing. He combines advice and a degree of prescription with a delineation of genre within the ethnographic cannon. Van Maanen does not enter into detailed discussion of textual conventions, but outlines types of 'story' that ethnographers typically recount. He distinguishes between 'realist', 'confessional' and 'impressionist' tales. The first type capitalizes on the traditions of realist reportage and fiction, inscribing the difference between the observer and the observed, and the relative disengagement of the researcher. It draws on a tradition of literary conventions that implicitly deny their conventionality. The tendency is to treat the text as an unproblematic representation of reality. The confessional is not really an alternative genre, since it is in a relation of complementarity rather than contrast. Ethnographers who have produced their realist accounts are frequently given to publishing autobiographical accounts in which the personal, the problematic and the narrative elements are in the foreground. For most authors, the confessional is contained within a separate account, and collections of such firsthand narrative of fieldwork experience have become a major sector in the published literature (For general examples of the type, see Bell and Encel 1978; Bell and Newby 1978; Bell and Roberts 1984; McKeganey and Cunningham-Burley 1987; Messerschmidt 1982; Whyte 1985. For recent examples that refer specifically to educational research see Burgess 1984, 1985a, 1985b, 1985c; Fetterman 1984; Spindler 1982; Walford 1988.) My own partial analysis of confessional accounts is contained in another of the essays in this volume. To some extent, therefore, the separation of the 'realist' and the 'confessional' accounts leaves the former relatively uncontaminated by the contingencies reflected in the latter. In Van Maanen's third type, the 'impressionist' tale, the entire account is permeated with a self-conscious deployment of the more 'literary' recources. The detachment of the realist genre is not sustained. The ethnography constructs a more explicitly vivid and metaphorical account. Van Maanen explores the characteristics of these alternatives, and commends a more explicit adoption of 'impressionist' approaches. He advocates -- and is not alone in this -- a more wholehearted recognition and celebration of the more 'literary' and metaphoric elements of ethnographic writing. Van Maanen's is a valuable contribution to the methodological literature. He may be faulted for over-stating the distinctions between the genres he identifies: all three may be found within the work of a single author, or indeed within the same monograph. Nevertheless, his provision of an accessible and systematic review will be a common reference point for students and their supervisors.

For further illumination one must also look to some recent texts that have been based on anthropological rather than sociological discourse. In recent years, cultural anthropologists in North America have become especially sensitive to the textual representation of anthropological work. They have drawn on semiotic and structuralist or poststructuralist theory to identify such issues as: the devices establishing the 'authority' of the text, and the 'narrative contract' between writer and reader; the writing of cultural 'difference' and the representation of the cultural 'other'; the self-representation of the ethnographer in the text. The range of analytic issues (by no means restricted to anthropological writing) are summarised by Clifford in the introduction to Clifford and Marcus (1986):

> Ethnographic writing is determined in at least six ways: (1) contextually (it draws from and creates meaningful social milieux); (2) rhetorically (it uses and is used by expressive conventions); (3) institutionally (one writes within, and against, specific traditions, disciplines, audiences); (4) generically (an ethnography is usually distinguishable from a novel or a travel account); (5) politically (the authority to represent cultural realities is unequally shared and at times contested); (6) historically (all the above conventions and constraints are changing). These determinations govern the inscription of coherent ethnographic fictions.

The deliberately challenging use of 'fictions' by authors in this vein is used to alert us to the *constructed* character of texts, whether they report, in the conventional sense, fact or fiction. As Clifford says in the same context, 'The making of ethnography is artisanal, tied to the worldly work of writing'.

The anthropologists, far more than the sociologists, have explored the textual nature of ethnographic writing as part of an epistemological and ideological crisis in the discipline. The agenda is in part political: the authority of the narrator is implicitly (but powerfully) claimed in the conventional style of ethnographic realism or ethnographic naturalism (cf Spencer 1989). That authority, moreover, rests on the textual construction of the *object* of description as 'the other' (cf Fabian 1983). Anthropological texts, it is claimed, present an unacceptably objectified account of a 'strange' culture: they transform the dialogues of fieldwork into a monologic, privileged account. Arguably, the anthropologists of this persuasion have become too thoroughly seduced by their own rhetoric of postmodernism. There is a danger of taking the literary-critical perspective too literally. As Spencer (1989) argues, by focusing too narrowly on the texts of anthropology, the contemporary critics themselves de-contextualise the work of writing from the other tasks of scholarship, including the tasks of fieldwork itself. Ironically for the discipline of anthropology, there is the parallel danger that the cultural and historical context of anthropological work is too readily reduced merely to phenomena of 'intertextuality'. Relations with other texts aand genres are important, but do not exhaust the intellectual and social context of their production or reception.

All genres, including the genres of scholarly, authoritative accounts, are rhetorically produced. The varieties of qualitative research, be they ethnographic, life-history, or ethnomethodological, all deploy characteristic conventions. It is part of their paradigm-like coherence that different styles of research are embodied in different styles of reportage. Now it is not the task for this paper to continue to review all the rapidly growing literature on these and related topics. Nor perhaps to reflect that for all the current work in this area, there remains scope for much more good work on the 'textual consrtruction of reality' in the social sciences. Rather, we need to reflect on some of the practical and methodological issues that face us as practitioners, supervisors and examiners.

Reflection into practice

It is easy to make the deceptively simple point that apprenticeship in the craft skills of writing is an essential element in research training. It is undeniable in principle that our students need to develop, and be helped to appreciate, the necessary disciplines for adequate writing. Books of advice and insight such as Richardson's (1990) provide an invaluable service in helping students and practitioners to reflect explicitly on their own and others' practices. Especially valuable from this perspective is Wolcott's synthesis of personal reflection and practical advice on the writing of ethnographic accounts (Wolcott 1990). It is vital to treat seriously the 'artisan' skills of textual construction, and much can be learned from the insights that experienced authors may share with their readers.. Many colleagues and students report finding Howard Becker's recent book an invaluable source of inspiration, sound advice and 'insider' wrinkles (Becker 1986). Students frequently need help to realise that writing is not easy for anybody; that their own shortcomings and blocks are not profound moral failings; that writing tasks can be approached as interesting intellectual puzzles; and so on. There are practical steps that can be taken to help on these and related matters. We can encourage groups of students to participate in writing workshops, in which mutual aid and sympathetic criticism are encouraged; where published texts are dissected and subjected to 'practical criticism'; where the organization of texts and draft passages are tried out with peers before being subjected to the scrutiny of a supervisor, an examiner or a journal's referees. These activities alone are difficult enough to achieve. They demand a social context of trust and mutual support: the most hardened can find the critical evaluation of their writing deeply threatening. Students have to be prepared to give time to each other rather than working in isolation. Through such activities students (and teachers) may also come to appreciate some of the more far-reaching intellectual implications.

As already indicated, the textual construction of qualitative research goes far beyond the problems of producing serviceable thesis drafts. The purpose of reflection is not just to encourage the production of more 'polished' writing (welcome though that always is). Rather, it should encourage the student group to understand their writing as encompassing methodological and analytic strategies. If we take seriously the thrust of recent work on the rhetoric and semiotics of ethnographic texts, then it is apparent that we cannot regard those texts as 'innocent'. It must become part of our reflexive self-awareness that we recognise the rhetorical and stylistic conventions with which we deal: not in order that textual analysis should substitute for fieldwork, but in order to bring it within our explicit methodological and epistemological understanding. Gone are the days when *writing* could be regarded as neutral. We have not yet reached the stage at which we can expect a shared understanding of our shared textual conventions.

The achievement of such a reflexive awareness is not easy, and in advocating it one is no doubt preaching an unattainable ideal (if ideal it be). For it requires an acquaintance with recent and contemporary literary theory, and with parallel work on the poetics of economics, history, law and so on. It suggests the development of collaborative relationships between social scientists and practitioners of 'literary' analysis. Nonetheless, I believe that it is worth cultivating at least some degree of critical reflection on the *form* of ethnographic writing as well as its content; the more that practitioners of qualitative research can cultivate such an informed understanding, the better students can be helped explicitly and self-consciously to deploy the literary conventions within which and against which they may formulate their work.

Furthermore, if we encourage our students to take explicit account of their textual practices, then we must recognise that this places on them a further burden. The more explicit and reflexive we render the methodology, the harder things get. It is easier to copy a taken-for-granted model than it is to understand the possibilities, to manipulate the conventions and to experiment with them. The latter is important. If we recognize that the conventional formats of 'realistic' reportage are essentially as arbitrary as any other, then we can open up the possibility to alternatives. Indeed, we may come to the view that the normal canons of written scientific discourse are inappropriate for the representation of complex and multiple social realities. Of course, we do not want to encourage a spate of modernist ethnographic texts (or whatever) just in order to promote novelty. But there is surely no harm in exploring alternative modes of representation in the light of an informed understanding of literary theory.

Some authors have made tentative steps in the direction of more self-conscious texts. Krieger (1979, 1983, 1984), for instance, claims quite explicitly to have written her ethnography taking 'stream of consciousness' novels as inspiration. Likewise, Bluebond-Langner (1980) employs dramatic conventions in presenting narrative and scenes. Both texts are noteworthy for trying to innovate rather than for any startling success. But the point is that some authors have tried. In recent years Michael Mulkay's uses of unusual textual genre (including the 'dialogue' form; parody; short story; and one-act play) make up the most sustained attempt to exploit the relationship between literary conventions and sociological arguments (e.g. Mulkay 1985). Indeed, in recent British sociology of science the use of 'new literary forms' has come to occupy a particular niche, equivalent to a theoretical or methodological sub-paradigm in the field. (For recent examples, see Woolgar 1988; Ashmore, Mulkay and Pinch 1989). Finally, there are two corollaries. First, if students are encouraged and able to explore such possibilities, then examiners must be willing to treat them seriously and sympathetically. (There are no extra marks for being gratuitously avant-garde, of course.) Secondly, the academy may need to be more open to masters and doctoral theses in which textual experimentation is a major raison d'etre; we cannot treat them as less important than any other methodological concerns.

5 Urban confessions

Introduction: the confessional

The purpose of this essay is to bring together some recent interests in the reading and writing ethnographic sociology and anthropology, and to apply one classic mode of analysis to texts of sociology. This essay is, therefore, intended as part of a rapidly growing literature on the literary and rhetorical devices available to the authors and readers of scholarly texts. Anthropologists have been in the forefront of various so-called 'new' approaches to texts of scholarship: sociologists - ethnographers in particular - are fast catching up (cf. Atkinson 1990, 1992). I focus here on one particular genre, and will try out one particular analytic strategy. The genre in question is the autobiographical or 'confessional' account, in which ethnographers 'tell it like it was' and reveal the personal and practical issues they experienced in the course of their own fieldwork. The genre is itself large and diverse, and growing steadily. Many ethnographers are impelled or invited to publish at least one such account from each fieldwork project. The autobiographical essay is a 'standard' output from ethnographic research. It is so much a taken-for-granted mode of writing that many fieldworkers must now be alert and sensitive to any potentially 'confessable' incidents in the course of their data collection and journal-keeping. All in the trade know that it is difficult not to think 'This will make a good story' in the course of field research - thinking either of incidents as 'data', or as memorable anecdotes for the revelatory account that must surely follow the safe publication of papers, monograph or whatever. The ethnographer who cannot generate personal anecdotes is in a sorry state indeed. The nature and form of those stories will form the substance of much of this chapter.

The following is not intended to be a comprehensive review of all ethnographic confessionals. The large and growing literature by cultural and social anthropologists on 'overseas' fieldwork experiences is not dealt with. To some extent, those accounts have been commented on already, directly or indirectly, in much of the recent work on the rhetoric of anthropology, though there remains much to be written on that anthropological genre. Likewise, no attempt has been made to include a comprehensive analysis of all sociologists' accounts. Again, there is now a substantial corpus, including different styles of narrative and reflection. The analysis outlined here can in due course be amplified and developed to incorporate, or contrast with, sources of different kinds. For the purpose of preliminary, exploratory analysis, the sources will be restricted to narrative accounts of fieldwork, primarily in urban settings. Consequently the approach does not include non-narrative accounts (such as those couched as advice to readers, or general reflections on personal response). There is no reason why a more comprehensive characterization of the genre and its varieties should not be built on lines indicated here, however.

In examining a corpus of ethnographic confessions, I shall use the formal analysis of narratives in the style initiated by the Russian formalist Vladimir Propp in his pioneering work on the morphology of the folk-tale (Propp 1968). It is an approach to narrative analysis that has been developed and extended by many subsequent authors, most notable those working in continental formalist, structuralist and post-structuralist traditions. I shall do this for heuristic purposes: the analysis will not be offered in the attempt to claim special and exclusive priority for such an approach. (Indeed, such formalist perspectives are currently rather unfashionable.)

It must be remembered that however 'intimate' and revealing confessionals may be, they are themselves artful products of writing. The genre is used by authors to invite particular kinds of readings and responses: the moral character and analytic acumen of the narrator are assembled out of the textual elements offered by the confessional. It would be quite wrong to assume that the 'confessional' embodies a 'true' and transparently unvarnished account, in contrast to the more worked-up 'realist' ethnographic text. There is nothing uniquely privileged or authentic about the autobiographical story. The confessional is as *conventional* as any other style or genre. Indeed, as the genre has grown in volume, so the contents and formats have become increasingly conventional. When the ethnographer reveals the 'inside story' of the research, then his or her narrative is as contrived as any other aspect of ethnographic writing. The observation is not intended to impugn the integrity of the individual authors in question, nor to call into question the validity of ethnographic research. The 'truth' is told in conventional ways; genre is not confined to fictional writing. It is, therefore, part of my purpose here to remind us that personal narratives of experience - whether they be by sociologists, anthropologists or other social actors, cannot be assumed to give us direct access to their innermost feelings and experiences. There is nothing privileged about the personal narrative, nothing uniquely personal. Like all acccounts, they are shaped by narrative and other conventions. They are therefore conventional in form, and culturally shaped.

The ethnographic confessional is, of course, a very well established genre.

In anthropology, sociology and educational research, numerous examples may be found in which the author purports to reveal 'the truth' and the personal experiences behind his or her published research. It is avowedly revelatory, and in embarking on such an account the author is frequently given to self-exposure. The confessional has most recently been commented on by Van Maanen (1988). He makes the obvious but important point that in the work of most authors, the 'confessional talk' stands opposed to the 'realist' mode of writing in which a dispassionate and relatively impersonal account is presented. In the main products of ethnographic research - monographs, articles, theses - there is greater stress in the writing on the 'observation' rather than the 'participation'. The personal elements are minimal:

> Basically, the narrator of realist tales poses as an impersonal conduit who, unlike missionaries, administrators, journalists, or unabashed members of the culture themselves, passes on more-or-less objective data in a measured intellectual style that is uncontaminated by personal bias, political goals, or moral judgements. A studied mentality characterizes the realist tale. (Van Maanen, 1988, p.47)

By contrast, the confessional tale is often published as a separate text, with a different style. They are concerned with the *personal*, often, indeed, the emotional aspects of fieldwork, and contrast with the realist mode:

> Confessionals do not usually replace realist accounts. They typically stand beside them, elaborating extensively on the formal snippets of method description that decorate realist tales. They occasionally appear in separate texts and provide self-explanatory and self-sealing accounts of how the author conducted a piece of research reported elsewhere. Confessions also appear, with increasing frequency, as separate articles, chapters of books devoted to fieldwork practice, or lengthy appendixes attached to realist monographs. All are distinct, however, from the ethnography itself. The confessional writings concern how the fieldworker's life was lived upriver among the natives. They are concerned primarily with how the fieldwork odyssey was accomplished by the researcher. There is then a clear break between the representation of the research work itself and the resulting ethnography (which appears elsewhere in the text or in another text altogether). Normally only the former is of concern in a confessional tale. (Van Maanen, 1988, p.75)

The confessional may, therefore, be viewed as a genre in its own right, often quite characteristically different from 'the ethnography' as an impersonal research report. Not only is there a substantial volume of published work in this vein, but there are also well established models and styles. Van Maanen writes about the authors' intentions, and the implications of confessional accounts. A recent phenomenon, he argues, they can have different - even dramatically opposed - epistemological justifications. On the one hand, the confessional mode can be used implicitly to justify the 'scientific' status of the ethnographic project: it warrants the credibility of the other published accounts. Because the 'messy' realities of fieldwork practice are divorced from the 'real' (and realist) ethnography, the appearance of the research itself can be sustained as independent of personalities, interests and the like. On the other hand, the confessional tale may be used to 'question the very basis of ethnographic authority'. They are used to represent the ethnographic project as a problematic one, shot through with ambiguity or uncertainty, and as a personal engagement, and as a contingent set of outcomes. The confessional autobiography is one way in which the ethnographer displays the capacity to reflect upon the ethnographic experience. Such reflection may be promoted as an aid to 'quality' control', in aspiring to the production of (conventionally define) valid and reliable accounts. They may therefore be justified in terms of public access to the research process in order to promote reproducible knowledge. Equally, they may celebrate not merely critical reflection, but the *reflexive* implication of the ethnographer with the social world that he or she reconstructs through field negotiations and dialogues.

While broad characterizations such as Van Maanen's do much to illuminate the general functions of autobiographical accounts, they leave unexplored their *form*. Yet, if there is now a recognisable genre of this type, then it makes sense to ask whether it is marked by any particular stylistic and organizational features: are there distinctive narrative structures and styles? Are there shared rhetorical devices that help to construct the 'confessional' mode? In what ways does the author portray him/herself in the text? What kind of implicit theoretical or methodological analyses and arguments are embedded in the accounts?

In the space of just one essay it is not possible, or even fruitful, to try to do justice to the full range of confessional and similar accounts that have now been written by sociologists, anthropologists and others. In order to examine some key features of the confessional genre I shall therefore confine my remarks to a relatively small number of texts. I shall examine a series of personal narratives in which urban sociologists or anthropologists describe their field experiences. They are all taken from American authors, and may be thought of as forming at least part of a relatively coherent corpus. There is a strong tradition of ethnographic work in American cities, stemming. of course, in no small part from the work of the early Chicago school of urban sociology. Many of the classic texts of American ethnography report research of this sort. I shall deal with a number of classic texts, including one

57

of the most famous of all confessionals, Whyte's methodological appendix to his *Street Corner Society*. That famous autobiographical account remains one of the most frequently cited accounts of fieldwork. That is so for at least two reasons, I suspect. First and foremost, it was one of the first extended accounts to provide an apparently unvarnished account of field research. Secondly, *Street Corner Society* was itself an important and widely read monograph. Whatever its empirical or methodological shortcomings, it has retained a place in the pantheon of modern sociological classics since its first publication. Moreover, the tradition of urban ethnography continues to flourish. Recent work, such as Duneier's prize-winning monograph *Slim's Table* (1992) is clearly in the tradition established by the Chicago school of urban studies, even in its resistance to some of that tradition's core traits. I am not so naive as to assume that parallels between Whyte's account and subsequent confessional are entirely contingent; nor that they can be explained only by reference to some general folk-model or Ur-text. Clearly Whyte's early contribution has found explicit and tacit echoes in subsequent writer's accounts. I do, however, suggest that we can understand this genre as a whole by paying close attention to some of its formal features. In doing so we shall discern some of the shared narrative conventions that help define this particular style of social-scientific writing. The specific corpus of texts to be examined is: *Street Corner Society* (Whyte 1981), *Tally's Corner* (Liebow 1967), *Soulside* (Hannerz 1969), *A Place on the Corner* (Anderson 1976), Wolf's reflections on his work among rebel bikers (Wolf 1991) and Van Maanen's own confessional (Van Maanen 1988). There are, of course, many confessionals, by sociologists, anthropologists, educational researchers and others, covering the study of small-scale societies, complex organizations, work settings, and a host of social worlds in general. I do not claim to have produced a model that is applicable equally to all those varieties of text.

Propp and the morphology of the tale

One preliminary approach to these and related issues, may be gained via a formalist account. We can - for heuristic purposes - treat the confessional genre as equivalent to the corpus of 'folk-tales' analysed by Propp in his pioneering analysis (Propp 1968). His structural approach, and that developed by subsequent commentators, may be used to identify the main forms and constituent elements. Propp subjected to analysis a very large number of Russian folk tales, and reduced their variety to a highly restricted set of elementary functions. The latter constitute the basic building-blocks of narrative structures. Each individual story realizes all or some of those functions in its own way: each story may thus be thought of as derived from the underlying set through processes of transformation and elaboration. In order to do full justice to the approach, one would ideally examine a substantial corpus of texts, as did Propp himself. A full analysis of all the autobiographical accounts published hitherto by anthropologists, sociologists and other fieldworkers would thus be the ideal approach. It would, however, require a much more lengthy treatment than is possible in this one essay. It must, therefore be acknowledged that here I sketch in the characteristic features of only one sub-genre. Propp derived four elementary propositions concerning the recurrent features of folk tales:

Functions of characters serve as stable, constant elements in a tale, independent of how and by whom they are fulfilled.
They constitute the fundamental components of a tale.
The number of functions known to the fairy-tale is limited.
The sequence of functions is always identical.
All fairy-tales are of one type in regard to their structure.
(Propp 1968, pp 21, 22, 23)

It remains to be seen whether a collection of such law-like generalizations can be claimed for the ethnographic confessional. There will be good grounds for suspecting less uniformity and less predictability than may be found within a folk corpus. Propp outlines a series of narrative elements and a set of character-functions. The roles are:

The villain
The donor
The helper
The princess (a sought-for person)
The dispatcher
The hero
The false hero

The narrative sequences are too long to reproduce in detail, but the following segment from the central section of the format illustrated the overall flavour of the analytic approach:

The hero leaves home
The hero is tested, interrogated or attacked.
The hero reacts to the actions of the future donor.
The hero acquires the use of a magical agent.
The hero is transferred, delivered, or led to the whereabouts of an object of search.
The hero and the villain join in direct combat.

There are thirty-one such narrative elements: they clearly resonate with any reader at all familiar with the folk-tale or fairy-story. Propp's approach gave rise to subsequent formalist approaches to literary and other texts, including, of course, the full-blown structuralist analyses of myth-logic in Levi-Strauss's mature structuralism.

In order to do justice to the approach it is necessary to study a corpus of related narratives rather than just single texts. For the purposes of this particular essay I shall deal with 'confessionals' of urban ethnography (broadly speaking), rather than those deriving from institutional settings, such as medicine, education, bureaucracies etc. Although that involves the inclusion of some texts that are so 'classic' as to be hackneyed, there are good reasons for limiting the scope. To a considerable extent, the classic urban texts have furnished models for many subsequent authors. They have, therefore, been especially important in shaping the genre.

Whyte's justly famous narrative of fieldwork experience in the Appendix to *Street Corner Society* (Whyte 1981) will therefore be used as a starting-point. Only halfhearted apologies are offered for the inclusion of such well known material: to the best of my knowledge it has not been analysed in quite this way before, and therefore some familiarity on the part of others may reasonably be assumed. It has the additional - very considerable - advantage that it is a very full account and therefore is likely to contain a wide variety of narrative elements that will be found in more fragmentary or incomplete form in briefer essays. In the event, it transpires that many of the narrative elements and characters to be found in Whyte's autobiographical account yield a repertoire of functions remarkably similar to Propp's folk-tale components. Indeed, viewed in this light, the ethnographic confessional starts to take on the appearance of a folk story in its own right.

It is difficult to arrive at a complete reading of Whyte's account and to summarize its narrative components in a comprehensive manner.   Here therefore I shall pick out some of the major and recurrent thematic elements. I have tentatively grouped them, and present below a partial summary:

Preparation and Upbringing
Ethnographer's personal background; upbringing different from
    culture in question.
College interests
Lack of experience; lack of preparation
Interest in site foreshadowed
Mistakes recognized
Influential book is read

First Attempts
Research opportunity
Choice of site; 'unscientific'
Ambitious research design
Advice from senior colleague; ambitious plans revised and
    abandoned.
Collaborator found
Advice from senior colleague
Unsatisfactory contact with the field research discontinued

Misleading advice from young colleague
Inappropriate entry to field; withdrawal

Getting Started
Point of entry via accident
Introduction to sponsor
Narrator and sponsor establish bargain
Help and advice on living arrangements
Narrator finds room with family
Becomes adopted by family

Getting Established
First occasion with sponsor; introduced to other actors
Avoids relations with females
Actors' curiosity; cover story for research
Sponsor becomes collaborator
Development of relationships and interactional skills
Doubts about research
Commits a blunder
Learns better approach
Blunder again
Modification of behavior
Divided loyalties
Key event establishes position

Apart from passages of retrospection and reflection, these seem to be the main elements in the opening narratives of Whyte's account. The whole Appendix contains many more components: some will be referred to later.

In the spirit of Propp's formal analysis one can already begin tentatively to identify some themes. First, there are the character-functions:

The ethnographer-hero
The adviser
The sponsor
The family
The false adviser

Of the major narrative functions one can begin to identify the following:

Hero's upbringing does not prepare him for the field
Makes unrealistic plans
Adviser helps to change plans
False adviser gives bad advice
Unsuccessful attempt to enter the field
Hero is rebuffed and withdraws from field

61

An unforeseen encounter provides point of entry
Hero makes contact with sponsor
Hero establishes new social relationships
Hero avoids inappropriate social relationships
Hero gains insight from a dramatic episode
Hero gains insight from a personal failing or blunder
Hero finds sanctuary with family (own or 'adopted')

While not definitive, these functions start to map out some of the formal properties of the tale, as told by Whyte. We have tentatively identified them from just part of one substantial narrative, of course.

Let us proceed by comparing this collection with the elements of a confessional account reporting a similar research experience - from Liebow's *Tally's Corner* (Liebow 1967). There Liebow provides an account of the genesis and development of his research: 'A Field Experience in Retrospect' (pp. 232-256). We should not expect the same number of functions, perhaps, as Liebow's is a much shorter tale than Whyte's. It is, nonetheless noticeable that some themes seem to recur. Here, then, is a summary of the Liebow account:

Hero's upbringing prepares him for the field
Receives advice and is sent out into field by adviser
Makes unrealistic plans
Unforeseen encounter provides entry to field
Hero meets sponsor
Establishes intimate relationships
Encounter suspicion and mistrust
Hero helps sponsor
Sponsor helps hero
Hero matches appearance to hosts

One can begin to discern some patterns of similarity and contrast between the two accounts. (The schematic summaries hide the greater complexity, richness and methodological sophistication of Whyte's account.)

The following extracts from *Soulside* (Hannerz 1969) provide yet further exemplification, and are used here to give more detailed versions of a number of themes. Hannerz gives us a fine example of the 'chance encounter' theme, after a period of unfocused and unproductive exploration. First, the wandering:

...I began to take walks in the neighborhood where I did not yet have any personal contacts; I preferred not to be sponsored there by the direct involvement of any other outsider....
After a few fruitless walks of this kind during which I was not yet ready to take any more abrupt steps toward contact, I came

upon a gathering of streetcorner men, one of whom called out to ask if I had a match. I did not, but I stopped to ask for the time, then went on to ask if they knew much about the neighborhood. (p.202)

Hannerz goes on to describe how he fell into conversation and shared some bottles of beer with the 'streetcorner men'. Again, in classic mode, the narrative moves to the introduction of the first named individual, who is to become a sponsor:

After a couple of hours of unevenly flowing conversation another man appeared and got into an argument with my new acquaintances. He was obviously quite intoxicated, and the exchange was loud. I was about to go home as he said to me, 'Don't sit here with those hoodlums, I'll let you meet some friends of mine'. This was Bee Jay....(p. 203)

One may note, incidentally, how important this initial encounter seems to be in the myth. Hannerz's total account occupies just ten pages. The narrative of the first day and its social relations occupies one and a half of them. Hannerz is by no means unusual in focusing on these 'first days in the field' to a disproportionate extent.

In Hannerz, as with others of the genre, the narrative of first meetings and consequent relationships is used to portray the research achievement as a natural and inevitable consequence of happy chance. Serendipity is thus translated into inevitability.

From the start at the street corner, I thus followed the natural links of social networks as I was introduced to more people. In this way I became rather readily acquainted with a great number of neighborhood people, as neighbors in daily interaction do not remain unaware of each others' friends, particularly not when these are as consistently present as I was. (p. 204)

Hannerz's account provides various passages concerning the theme of identity and difference. For instance:

The first evening...the conversation of the gathering soon turned to Swedish topics.... Thus my emergent identity soon seemed to be Swedish first, some-kind-of-fellow-who-wants-to-know-about-the-neighborhood-and-maybe-write-a-book-about-it second.... Already, this evening a mispronunciation of my first name became stabilised, and this was the name by which I became known in the following period. (p. 203)
... there was little likelihood that I would ever manage not to be

conspicuous wherever I was. Bee Jay suggested jokingly that I might be the real 'blue-eyed blond devil' the Muslims were talking about. But at least I could try not to make my behavior seem equally out of place. I dressed informally in order not to look like those whites who are only in the ghetto 'on business', and although Fats once asked if he could exchange his thirty-dollar hat for mine, my clothes were not generally anything out of the ordinary - the hat in question was from a dime store. I also tried to change my speech in the direction of the ghetto dialect, although I knew I would not be able to master its complexity very easily. Of course I could not become like a ghetto dweller. (pp. 206-7)

Hannerz's marginal, outsider position places him in an exposed, even dangerous position:

... obviously even a very innocent remark could be seen in an unexpected light. Jimmy, for instance, noted before for his hot temper, was upset when I made a complimentary remark about his new sweater and asked where he had got it.

'What the hell do you mean, where did I get it? This is my own sweater, I bought it. Why do you ask? I don't know if we can trust you'.

Ribs, one of the first men I met in the neighborhood, also turned out to be very suspicious as I encountered him one evening on the street when I was speaking with Sonny and Carl. He had been away from the neighborhood almost since we first met, so at this time he had less of an idea why I was there than most people. After telling me that he did not want to have me around he threatened to cut my throat some time; at that moment a policeman walked past on his beat, and Ribs left. (pp. 209-10)

At this point we can turn from the first three, closely related, texts to consider a slightly different exemplar. Van Maanen's account of his own research experiences is not a full narrative of his fieldwork activities (and Van Maanen is perhaps the least naive of all confessional authors). It includes some confessional accounts of his work with urban police officers. While not strictly part of the same canon, it would be silly to ignore it: not least because Van Maanen uses his own experiences self-consciously to illustrate the confessional style in his more general discussion of ethnographers' tales. It is noticeable that it contains several of the 'classic' elements. It begins, for instance, with a quote from his original dissertation proposal, showing how poorly it actually guided the subsequent research on police work. Equally characteristically, Van Maanen (1988) indicates his own biographical motivation:

> ... I also had grown up subject to what I regarded as more than
> my share of police attention and hence viewed the police with a
> little loathing, some fear, and considerable curiosity. Nor were
> such feelings devoid of analytic suppposition. I did not go into
> the field out of affection for the police. In many ways, I had it in
> for them as I packed my bags. (p.33)

He also writes particularly tellingly of the various 'trials' and initiations
undergone in the line of ethnographic work:

> In the beginning, I was provided a uniform, a reservist badge and
> number, a departmental issue .32-caliber revolver, and a slot in
> the police academy training class. (p.37)

In that vein he writes about a 'balls test' -- the assessment of a rookie's
capacity to support a fellow officer -- and how it was applied to him:

> There were instances ... where I felt it necessary to assist -- in
> police parlance, to back up -- the patrolmen I was ostensibly
> observing. At such moments, I was hardly making the rational,
> reasoned choice in light of the instrumental research objectives I
> had set. (p.38)

He also notes that in the police academy he seemed to attract more than his
fair share of punishments, which he submitted to. In common with the other
examples already referred to, Van Maanen provides testimony as to the trials
and tribulations (including physical danger) that he was subject to in the
course of his protracted field research among the police. Of course, his
continued involvement and successful completion of the research is also
evidence of his success in overcoming those troubles.

A much more recent example of the urban ethnographer's Odyssey is
provided by Wolf (1991), in an essay that explicitly and self-consciously
plays up the personal and intellectual danger of an ethnographic project. (The
title of the paper - 'High Risk Methodology" - is revealing, if appropriate,
given that the subject-matter was Outlaw Bikers.) Some of the common
motifs can be identified and illustrated further.

The Hero's personal background:

> Brought up in the streets of a lower-class neighborhood, I saw
> my best friend - with whom I broke into abandoned buildings as
> a kid - sent to prison for grand theft auto, and then shot down in
> an attempted armed robbery. Rather than be crushed like that, I
> worked in meat-packing plants and factories for 13 hours a day

so that I could buy myself a British-made Norton motorcycle and put myself through university.... believe that it was this aspect of my nonacademic background - the fact that I had learned to ride and beat the streets - that made it possible for me to contemplate such a study, and eventually to ride with the Rebels. (p.213)

The Hero fails in an early attempt:

...I lacked patience and pushed the situation by asking too many questions. I found out quickly that outsiders, even bikers, do not rush into a club, and that anyone who doesn't show the proper restraint will be shut out.... Days later I carelessly got into an argument with a club 'striker', a probationary member, that led to blows in a barroom skirmish. He flattened my nose and began choking me. Unable to get air down my throat and breathing only blood through my nostrils, I managed a body punch that found his solar plexus and loosened his grip. I then grabbed one of his hands and pulled back on the thumb until I heard the joint break. (p.213)

The Hero changes appearance:

I fine-tuned my image before I approached the Rebels...I purchased an old 1955 Harley-Davidson FL ... but later sold (it) in favor of a mechanically more reliable 1972 Electraglide ... I had grown shoulder-length hair and a heavy beard. I bought a Harley-Davidson leather jacket and vest, wore studded leather wristbands and a shark's tooth pendant, and sported a cutoff denim jacket with assorted Harley-Davidson pins and patches, all symbolic of the outlaw biker worldview.(p.214)

A chance encounter leads Hero to a Helper:

[Wolf is trying to figure out how to approach the Rebels, at the 'Kingsway Motor Inn'].... I had thought through five different approaches when Wee Albert of the Rebels MC came out of the bar to do a security check on the 'Rebel Iron' in the parking lot. He saw me leaning on my bike and came over to check me out. For some time Wee Albert and I stood in the parking lot and talked about motorcycles, riding in the wind, and the Harley tradition. He showed me some of the more impressive Rebel choppers and detailed the jobs of customizing that members of the club had done to their machines. He then checked out my 'hog', gave a grunt of approval, and then invited me to come in and join the Rebels at their tables. (p.215)

The Helper introduces the Hero:

> Wee Albert became a good buddy of mine, and he sponsored my participation on club runs and at club parties.... The number of close friends that I had in the club increased and I was gradually drawn into the biker brotherhood. (p.215)

The Hero undergoes various tests and dangers:

> To a patch holder, brotherhood means being there when needed; its most dramatic expression occurs when brothers defend each other from outside threats. I vividly remember sitting with the Rebels in the Kingsway Motor Inn bar, trying to sober up quickly while I mentally acted out what I thought would be my best martial-arts moves. I looked down at my hand; I had sprained my thumb the night before while sparring in karate. My right hand was black, blue, swollen, and useless. I watched nervously as 65 members of the Canadian Airborne Regiment strutted into the bar. Their walk said that they were looking for us and a brawl. I came to view brotherhood as both a privilege and a tremendous personal responsibility. (p.216)

The Hero develops close relationships:

> Gradually my status changed from being a biker with a familiar face to being a friend of the club. There were no formal announcements; Tiny just yelled across at me one afternoon while we were starting up our bikes, 'Hey! Coyote! No way am I riding beside you. Some farmer is going to shoot our arses off and then say he was shooting at varmints.' (Wolf is given the nickname 'Coyote' - a reference to the coyote skin he had taken to wearing over his helmet.) (pp. 216-217)

Here again, then, one can see the classic themes in Wolf's somewhat dramatic account of his fieldwork experiences. It recapitulates many of the narrative elements and functions that I have identified already. I have used extracts from it to illustrate the essay, rather than present it solely in summary form, partly because it will be much less familiar to most readers than the other texts I have referred to, and partly to show that a contemporary publication continues the tradition. I now go on to consider two further features of the genre. To begin with I examine some of the underlying structural oppositions to be found encoded in these texts. I then go on to consider a partial counter-example, which has some of the key narrative functions noticeably absent.

Contrasts

One of the noticeable features about the narrative functions that can be identified throughout the corpus (though not necessarily in each individual text) is the fact that many of them partake of categories of *contrast*. They can be linked by grouping them into binary oppositions. The systemic relationships of similarity and difference thus allow us to build an armature: a discursive space within which the narrative of discovery is produced and read. They reflect underlying oppositions within the corpus of 'folk-tales', which in turn imply fundamental antinomies.

Recurrent oppositions are:

True helpers	False helpers
Planned purposeful action	Accident
Initiation of social relations	Avoidance of social relations
Trust	Suspicion
Safety	Danger
Cultural similarity	Cultural difference
Innocence	Sophistication
Confusion	Understanding
Family present	Family absent
Aceptance	Rejection

Of course, at one level, it comes as no great surprise to learn that the autobiographical accounts of sociologists and anthropologists 'in the field' in urban settings are imbued with some of these themes: separation, danger, intimacy and strangeness. They are - or at least they have become - part of the culture of fieldwork itself. It is, however, striking that the field itself (the corpus of texts, that is) is quite so predictably patterned and structured.

The narratives and recollections do indeed have some affinities with classic folk tales. It is not difficult, in fact, to re-cast the ideal-typical ethnographic autobiography as a folk-tale.

The hero's biographical background;
Hero decides to go (or is dispatched) into the field;
Hero embarks on the quest;
Makes over-ambitious or unrealistic plans;
Receives advice from Adviser;
Hero embarks on the quest afresh;
Hero makes tentative and/or unsuccessful attempts to gain entry;
A chance encounter leads hero to a Helper;
The Hero encounters various tests and dangers;
The Helper guides the Hero through various difficulties;
The Helper reveals hidden knowledge;

The Hero changes his appearance;
The Hero learns new language;
and so on.

Indeed, the sociological-cum-anthropological 'confessional' takes on an archetypal quality. It has these obvious affinities with 'quest' tales that are ancient in origin and of universal their distribution. For all his or her trials, tribulations, false hopes, unfulfilled ambitions and incomplete achievement, the ethnographer can thus portray the narrator as an archetypical Hero of sorts. He or she is not, however, the hero to whom all things come readily, who conquers all and is invulnerable. The classic type is rather that of Odysseus, whose main attribute in the Homeric epics was captured in the epithet 'polytropos' - a term that captures his wily resourcefulness. For the Hero of the ethnographic confessional is, mythologically speaking, both Hero and Trickster. (To return to the formalist reading outlined above, one could argue that the person of the ethnographer realises both narrative functions - sometimes simultaneously).

That very point has been made already, in a different analytic context, by Van Maanen (1988: 76), who writes: 'The ethnographer as the visible actor in the confessional tale is often something of a trickster or fixer, wise to the ways the world, appreciative of human vanity, necessarily wary, and therefore inventive at getting by and winning little victories over the hassles of life in the research setting...'. The 'trickster' image is, of course, congruent with many of the desired self-images of the ethnographer, and with the ideals of ethnographic method. The fieldworker who strives to establish a social position of 'marginal native' or some such designation - will likely celebrate the twists and turns of ambiguity. The preferred self-portrait will therefore find the ethnographer poised between the mythological polarities: of intimacy and distance, familiarity and strangeness, involvement and disengagement, understanding and incomprehension. The 'quest' will turn and turn again within a framework of 'insider' and 'outsider', knowledge and ignorance.

It is not necessary to compare the tales of the ethnographers with distant or exotic folktales. It is instructive to compare my own analysis of their narratrive functions with Wright's analysis of the classic Western film. The functions of the Western are:

The hero enters a social group
The hero is unknown to society
The hero is revealed to have an exceptional ability
The society recognizes the difference between themselves and
    the hero, who is given special status
The society does not completely accept the hero
There is a conflict of interest between the villains and society
The villains are stronger than society
There is a strong friendship or respect between the hero and the

villain
The villains threaten society
The hero avoids involvement in the conflict
The villains endanger a friend of the hero
The hero fights the villains
The hero defeats the villains
The society is safe
The society accepts the hero
The hero loses or gives up his special status.

(Wright 1975: 48-49)

Naturally, the ethnographer-as-hero does not normally have to defeat villains in quite the way that The Lone Ranger or a John Wayne character might, although he or she has to overcome fearful tribulations. They are sometimes caused by suspicious or even hostile characters, but the show-downs are rarely marked by gunplay or other physical violence. But the sense of heroic obligation, the hard-worn acquisition of special insight and status, coupled with the position of marginality, all have echoes with the Western narrative. That is not altogether surpirising: we have relatively few conventions for the expression of heroic status. In a similar vein, the ethnographer's quest for knowledge and wisdom could be compared more formally with other quests for enlightenment, and the trials that normally beset the seeker or pilgrim. Clearly there are affinities with such narratives as *Pilgrim's Progress*, *The Magic Flute*, or *Parsifal*.

It would be wrong to assume that all autobiographical accounts of the research process are identical, even where there are close affinities in the substance and style of research. Even when there are strong generic similarities, there may be differences, and those differences may themselves be highly illuminating. If we restrict ourselves to the formal analysis outlined above for the moment, it is worth noting that the presence or absence of a given narrative function or element may be quite significant for the overall reception of the text. In analyses of the sort I have attempted here, it is always dangerously easy to imply that all the relevant texts conform exactly to the one structure or ideal type. Yet counter-examples are always important, not least because their apparent deviation from the more common pattern may have narrative functions in its own right. An interesting case here is the opening account of Elijah Anderson's *A Place on the Corner* (Anderson 1976). This is clearly a canonical work. It derives from a Chicago PhD, acknowledges major figures in urban sociology; and the blurb on the back cover quotes from reviewers who place the book firmly in the tradition of Whyte, Suttles, Liebow and Hannerz, amongst others. Yet there are some clear differences in narrative structure and point of view that are indexed by the presence and absence of narrative functions.

At the outset it is clear that there are elements present in Whyte, Liebow and Hannerz that are absent from Anderson. Unlike them he has no

70

statement as to his own identity or socialization: there is no reference to the congruence or otherwise of his ethnicity and upbringing with those of his hosts. Secondly, the elements relating to advisers and mentors are not there. The early episodes found in Whyte and Liebow, concerning the original research design and the advice of senior colleagues are just not there. Thirdly, the processes of approach, of tentative first steps towards the research site, are almost totally absent. Hence the section entitled 'Getting In' (p.7) begins as follows:

My first few weeks at Jelly's were spent on the barroom side among the visitors and others. This side ... was the place most accessible to new people, where strangers could congregate. It was also a place where I could be relatively unobtrusive, yet somewhat sociable. It was here that the process of getting to know Jelly's began, where increasingly I gained some license to exist and talk openly with people. Initially this meant getting to know the people and becoming somewhat involved in their relationships with one another; becoming familiar with the common, everyday understandings people shared and took for granted, the social rules and expectations they held for one another. (pp. 7-8)

Anderson then goes on to reconstruct one of his early encounters, with a man named Clarence - illustrating 'both the potential for intimacy and the transience characterizing a great many relations among visitors on the barroom side' (p.8). It is noteworthy that prior to this section on 'getting in', Anderson has *already* introduced the setting of his ethnography:

'Jelly's', the subject of this study, is a bar and liquor store located in a run-down building on the south side of Chicago. Situated at a corner of a main thoroughfare, Jelly's is a hangout for working and nonworking, neighborhood and nonneighborhood black people, mostly men. (p. 1)

Anderson goes on to describe the immediate locale surrounding Jelly's, and gives a brief introduction to the interior of Jelly's itself.

What is remarkable about Anderson's narrative, then, is not just the absence of some (presumably optional) narrative components, but the potential effect on the reader. For, put in a rather more positive way, the opening of the autobiographical introduction has a particular force. Jelly's is 'there' - it is not, as it were, stumbled into - and Anderson is 'there'. He is not encountered as an outsider navigating his way into the setting and coming across his final research site. He and it are introduced with equal self-assurance. Coupled with an almost complete lack of reference to either personal or academic background, Anderson's presence in the setting is

71

treated remarkably unproblematically. What we might call the context of strangeness or outside status is totally absent.

Anderson does not say so explicitly. It is, therefore, left to the reader to infer that Anderson is *not* 'out of place' here, at least to the extent that he is himself black. Consequently, one of the 'standard' narrative functions - the finding of a 'sponsor' or helper takes on a particular force in Anderson's account. He recounts his initial encounter with Herman, a forty-five-year-old janitor. Herman is different from the people already encountered by Anderson - for his is not just a 'visitor', but a regular at Jelly's. Herman inquires what Anderson is doing there, and by a process of mutual interrogation Herman and Anderson begin to establish their acquaintance, and establish the relationship that will allow Anderson to be sponsored into the local social networks.

> In response to Herman's inquiries about my occupation, I said, "I'm a graduate student over at the University of Chicago". "That's nice", said Herman, seeming a little surprised. How long you been over there?" As I answered his questions, he seemed to take this as a kind of license to ask more and more about me. And I took his inquiries as cues that I could do the same. Taking this license, I asked him more about himself. During this exchange of information I noticed a marked change in Herman's demeanor toward me. He became more relaxed and sure of me. He gestured more as he spoke, punctuating his words with hits and jabs to my shoulder. He was a very friendly and affable man. At times I reciprocated by punctuating my own words with smiles and friendly exclamations. On the ghetto streets and in ghetto bars friendly students are not to be feared and suspected but are generally expected to be "square" and bookish. With all the information he had about me, including my willingness to give it, he could place me as "safe" within his own scheme of standards and values. (p.13)

It is, therefore, noteworthy that the theme of 'family' or 'kinship' is a central one here. Whyte, it will be recalled, had become 'adopted' by his Italian-American family. Anderson is invited to enter into an even more overt and intimate relationship of fictive kinship. Herman has invited Anderson to accompany him to a Christmas party.

> When I arrived at his place of work on the day of the party, Herman showed me around the buildings he kept clean as janitor. He led me from room to room, from hallway to hallway, and from floor to floor, taking great pride in their immaculate look. As he showed me around, he said in an aside that he would have to introduce me to others as his "cousin", since he could not let

"just anybody" in there. I agreed to be his "cousin", which was still a dubious status in the minds of those we were to encounter at the party, if not in Herman's own mind. But this was Herman's show. He was the director. (pp. 17-18)

The section is sub-titled 'Going for Cousins'.

The passages describing the initial encounter with Herman and the party occupy a substantial proportion of Anderson's autobiographical narrative. For the rest he described 'working at sociability', especially the necessity for him to 'read the signs', of self-presentation and personal style in and around Jelly's. In common with other first-person narratives Anderson includes the narrative component of 'difficult' or 'threatening' situations, where his sponsor looks out for him:

It was a balmy Saturday evening in April. Herman, Leroy, Charlie, Tony and I were standing in front of Jelly's liquor-store window. An ice-cold can of Budweiser, wrapped in a brown paper sack, changed hands. Each man took a swig and passed the can on. Cars and buses passed by and their passengers glanced over, but the men were oblivious to this. Pedestrians quickly moved on. An old flea-bitten brown mutt limped by. Tony was in a playful mood and began poking me in the side. The poking soon turned into shoulder-bumping. Herman, who had been watching this, said to Tony, in a half-kidding yet firm way, "Why don't you cut all that weak shit, Tony". Tony stopped at what was taken as a warning from Herman. (p. 25)

We have seen how Whyte, Liebow and Hannerz comment on their changing linguistic behavior. A similar narrative element appears in Anderson, but again with an interesting variation. To begin with, he remarks on the changing behavior of his sponsor when interacting with particular individuals. For instance; they encounter Oscar, "a fast, street-wise former street-gang member of thirty-three who is now a hustler on the streets" (p.26):

Herman and Oscar exchanged a few words, as Herman moved astutely and almost effortlessly to Oscar's "level" by his speech and demeanour. Herman spoke "hip street shit", spiced with a few "mother-fuckers", "son' bitches", or whatever it took. I just sat at the bar with my beer in hand and watched Herman in action. (p. 27)

Anderson refers to this as an "exhibition" between the two men. Anderson is then introduced to Oscar as Herman's cousin Eli,

"Hey, brother-man. What's to it?" said Oscar, as he extended his hand to me for a social handshake. "You", I responded, as I shook his hand. (p. 27)

Here, then. Anderson does *not* mention any conscious effort on his part to learn new language or modify his behavior. By implication he has slipped into a 'soul brother' mode. Unlike the reported experiences of Whyte, Leibow or Hannerz, this is not an uncomfortably self-conscious activity; nor is it something that called for any comment from his sponsor or other hosts (unlike Doc's comment on Whyte's change of self-presentation).

To summarise, therefore: Anderson's autobiographical account of the research includes some of the 'stock' narrative themes, while giving them a particular twist, and omits others. The net effect is to transform the 'point of view' of the account quite radically. Whyte, Liebow, Hannerz and others can be read as offering the story of a 'guest'. The outsider overcomes vicissitudes and becomes an accepted insider; blunders are learned from, dangers overcome; ignorance is supplanted by competence and understanding. Anderson's account is tellingly different. Jelly's is not discovered, or visited, or selected as a research site: it is *there*. Anderson himself embarks on no quest. He does not tentatively embark on the field research; he apparently makes no mistakes; he too is *there*. The narrative themes he employs therefore omit the 'bracketing' functions of the 'outsider' and his adjustments. The surface similarity of the narrative to others of the genre in fact masks the fact that its point of view is almost diametrically opposed to theirs. There is in Anderson remarkably little of the ambiguity to be found in the other accounts.

Conclusion

The sociological ethnographer who studies a segment of his or her own culture, such as a major city, may find a certain ambiguity and feel a certain reticence in expressing this mythology of the quest. The anthropologist who studies suitable exotic and alien cultures may have little difficulty in composing satisfyingly dramatic and vivid accounts of the quest. The stories may be evocatively spiced and loaded with tales of hardships, deprivation, privation, danger and fortitude. These may be presented with a certain patrician aloofness and detachment, such as Evans-Pritchard's accounts (Geertz 1983) or with a liberal dose of self-mockery and broad humour, as in Nigel Barley's more recent contributions to the anthropological genre (e.g. Barley 1983). Nevertheless, the literary models of intrepid exploration may continue to exert their influence. The isolation and the vicissitudes will still be understood as real enough by the sympathetic reader.

For the urban ethnographer of modern Britain or America things are a bit less obvious. There may indeed be discomforts and dangers, but they do not normally quite match the anthropologist's. The urban sociologist cannot quite take on the anthropologist whose canoe overturns so that all her possessions are lost or destroyed. After all, the reader and the author know that he or she can pop into the local K-Mart and keep body and soul together. As one author (Rosenberg 1988: xi)), writing about another field setting, has commented:

> I loved living in France and was amused when my anthropologist colleagues who worked in more exotic locales, asked about my time in the bush. I would bravely attempt to match their stories of hardship by pointing out that 'my village' was more than twenty-four hours away from the nearest three-star restaurant.

If urban ethnographers have any implicit literary parallels for their accounts, then it is not the voyage of discovery, the trek upcountry and the expedition to the interior. Nevertheless, urban ethnographers *can* recount a quest. They have available to them narrative formats and models through which their experiences may be conveyed. It is not necessary to question the veracity of urban confessions in order to draw attention to the conventional ways in which (some of them) have been couched. It is, however, naive to subscribe to the view that such autobiographical accounts are any less contrived or more authentic than any other genre of sociological reportage.

6 At Man's Best Hospital and the Mug'n'Muffin

Introduction

> As we went over the Mass. Ave. Bridge I looked at the way the
> rain dimpled the surface of the river. The sweep of the Charles
> from the bridge down towards the basin was very fine from the
> Mass. Ave. Bridge - much better when you walked across it, but
> okay from a car. The red-brick city on Beacon Hill, the original
> one, was prominent from here, capped by the gold dome of the
> Bulfinch State House. The high-rises of the modern city were all
> around it, but from here they didn't dominate. It was like looking
> back through the rain to the way it was and maybe should have
> been. (Parker, 1982: 50)

Robert Parker's novels conjure up many such visions of Boston and
Cambridge, the scene of my trials and embarrassments as a novice facing
American medicine. This paper is an account of two key episodes in my
early days of living and working in the United States (as opposed to visiting
as a tourist) and can be read as a contribution to three sorts of literature by
social scientists: medical sociologists' accounts of their own experiences of
health and illness (e.g. Horobin and Davis, 1977); that on 'lay' and
'professional' understandings of health states and the social distribution of
knowledge (e.g. Comaroff, 1982; Hughes, 1976; Murcott, 1981; Posner,
1976; Strong 1980); and anthropologists' and sociologists' autobiographical
accounts of their fieldwork experiences (e.g.Hammond, 1964; Bell and
Newby, 1977).

This essay falls into three main sections. Following a brief introduction,
giving some background to the experiences described, comes an account of
my first encounter with the professional face of medicine in America. This is
followed by an encounter with the lay side of American medicine at the Mug
'n' Muffin. The final section is a reflection on the *genre* of confessional

accounts by social scientists, focusing on their underlying motivation, style and audience.

Background

The incidents described in this essay took place in the Fall of 1984, when I was on sabbatical leave from Cardiff and attached to Boston University (one of the 40 or so Universities and Colleges in the Greater Boston area), and to one of the many teaching hospitals in the city. Borrowing from Shem's novel *House of God* (1978) I have called it Man's Best Hospital (MBH). My research plan, negotiated with Duncan McKay (a pseudonym), a senior clinical professor at the MBH, was that I should undertake an intensive ethnography of the work of haematologists for a period of ten weeks - from early October to mid December. My focus was not unrelated to my previous research in teaching hospitals (e.g. Atkinson, 1976, 1977a, 1977b, 1977c, 1981, 1984a, 1984b). I was again interested in the construction and transmission of medical knowledge. Now I was less preoccupied with medical education *per se* than with the production and distribution of expert knowledge within and between specialities. I planned to focus on haematologists because I wanted to see how 'scientific' findings of the laboratory entered into clinical decision-making at the bedside and on the ward. It had been agreed that I would spend most of my time following the clinical fellows in haematology (that is, junior doctors following post-residency specialist training).

The access to the MBH had been easier than my Scottish research, where negotiations to gain permission to observe clinical teaching on the wards took a year in all. At the MBH my chief sponsor had invited me to do research there when we met briefly at the Social Science and Medicine conference held in Stirling in July 1983, partly because he had enjoyed the monograph based on my Ph.D. (Atkinson, 1981). I accepted the invitation, and visited Cambridge and Boston in March 1984 to see Duncan McKay again, and make provisional arrangements for the sabbatical. I needed agreement from the haematologists, and an attachment to a social science department in one of the relevant universities. The Head of Haematology at MBH, Hamilton Peacock, had interviewed me in March and was agreeable. My attachment to BU was also arranged in 1984, thanks to George Psathas and John McKinlay. Accordingly, I flew from Heathrow to Boston on October 2nd 1984, and on the morning of October 5th I began the final round of negotiations for access at the MBH and with the particular individuals I hoped to accompany on their ward rounds, case conferences and meal breaks for the next ten weeks.

The data on which this chapter is based come from a field diary I kept while I was in Boston, supplemented by the letters I wrote home. As an experienced medical sociologist and ethnographer many aspects of the Boston episode were familiar, but equally many features of American life and medicine were strange. Boston itself was not unfamiliar. I had attended the ASA there in 1979 as well as the week in Cambridge in March 1984 making provisional arrangements for the sabbatical. Thus, when I arrived in October 1984 I had completed the basic access negotiations, was vaguely familiar with the urban geography and public transport systems of Boston and Cambridge, and had seen the inside of the BU Sociology Department and the MBH. As ever, none of this had prepared me for my first day in the field.

Encountering American medicine at Man's Best Hospital

On the evening of October 5th I wrote home to Cardiff to the effect that

> I've now been into the MBH, where I'm now officially a member of staff. This turned out to be more complex than I'd expected....

Behind this statement lay a series of encounters which underlined my status as an incompetent outsider, and which I recorded as faithfully as I could in my field diary. It had been agreed that I was to have the splendid title of Honorary Consultant in Sociology, Division of Medicine at MBH. This would entitle me to the magic identity badge which, when pinned to my breast pocket, would allow me to wander unmolested in the hospital. When I left Cardiff the final confirmation of this appointment had not yet come through. I had thought it would involve some very minor bureaucratic work, but it wasn't quite as simple as I had envisaged. My field diary takes up the story....

> *October 5th*
> As arranged on the phone yesterday, today I have an appointment to see Dr. Peacock. In the morning I phone Linda Erwinger (an administrative assistant at MBH who has been dealing with my appointment) to let her know that I am coming in, and to ask if she has any news of my appointment as consultant. She tells me it has been approved and I should go to the Registrar's office to get my ID - as without it I can't really get very far in the hospital. She explains that I need to go to the office on the first floor of the Cabot Building. As usual, I have to make a conscious effort to remember that the 'first floor' is the 'ground floor' in real English. I tell her I'll see her in the early afternoon. She has the pleasant manner and telephone voice I am coming to accept as normal in American organizations. [Later I will come to associate the general style with bureaucratic inefficiency and being given the run around: the *appearance* of courteous efficiency belies the horrible truth of most American people-processing organizations.] I have made a late start to the day, as I am still sleepy and a bit jet-lagged. I debate whether to

go to the MBH early or to wait. I decide to go, and as it turns out this is a lucky decision. I make a fairly leisurely way to the hospital, getting off the T a couple of stops early and walking through attractive residential streets in the autumn sun. [The 'T' is local shorthand for the MBTA, the urban transit system run by the Massachusetts Bay Transport Authority.]

I am surprised at how readily I recall the hospital and its layout: I find the Registrar's office almost immediately. A pretty girl called Petra searches the files and finds the confirmation of my appointment. She sits me down and makes me fill out a couple of forms. Predictably, I don't know half the things asked for - such as which service or department I should put down, or where I am to be working etc., etc. This doesn't seem to matter very much, and I suppose that for a very short-term visiting, unpaid appointment it isn't regarded as too important. Petra explains that I need to get my Unit Number: I can't do anything without that. She doesn't explain exactly what it is and I do not ask for clarification. She writes out a form for me to take with me; it is a general set of instructions for new staff and fellows. She explains that - as the latter states - I need to take my Unit Number to Staff Records on the Second Floor of the Cabot Building. (The form letter adds sternly 'be sure to have either Appointment Letter or Form Letter from Registrar's office with you'.) There I am to obtain an ID form which I then take to Security on the first [ground] floor of the Greene Building, to have my picture taken. Petra explains that I cannot do these latter tasks until Tuesday, as the relevant offices only process IDs on Tuesdays.

In the meantime, she admires my onyx ring. I take it off and explain how it was made for me by a friend in Cardiff who is a professional jeweller. Petra says she always thought onyx would make the perfect engagement ring. I reply that 'I promise that when I propose this will be the ring I offer'. Petra tries it on her finger anyway.

These pleasantries over I pad off, as directed, to the staff clinic. I poke my head in the door so marked, and they tell me to start in the office on the other side of the corridor. I go there, and the young woman inside hands me a pair of daunting looking forms. I start to look round for somewhere to sit, but as I tentatively make towards a corner of her office she curtly tells me to take a clip-board from the shelf and go outside to sit in the corridor. I am therefore already feeling a bit sheepish before I sit down. Soon, as I scan the forms, I start to feel thoroughly inadequate. It turns out that a detailed and rather specific medical inventory is requested, plus some personal details which seem irrelevant or less than easy to comply with.

Of course, I can give my name, date of birth ... but even with the basic face-sheet data things are tricky. My address, for instance. I haven't got a permanent address in Boston, and it seems a bit silly to give one which will have to be changed in about six weeks time. (And 'no fixed abode' is hardly conducive of trust...) So I put c/o Department of Sociology, BU etc.. Since I can't remember the phone number for there, or anywhere else for that matter, I leave that blank. (Later I shall learn that the lack of a telephone number is a greater social handicap by far than the lack of a suitable address.) Then 'who is your personal physician?'. Oh Lord! Do they demand I register with a physician in Boston? I haven't, that's for sure, and don't really want to. It crosses my mind that if I have to, then he (or she) will probably insist on a full medical, no doubt at considerable cost. Will Accident and General cover such non-emergency costs? It seems unlikely. I put down my own GP in Cardiff and hope this will do. If it takes as long as this to contemplate and answer every question, then it will take all day and I'll be late for my appointment with Dr. Peacock. Will it be possible to break off this bureaucratic process for the appointment, or must it run its course inexorably? I strongly suspect the latter, and try to buckle down to my task.

My weight. This is easier - at least I know it in round terms. But how to report it? I know most Americans report weight in pounds only; but maybe kilos would be more appropriate for the medical profession. If I get the arithmetic wrong, then I'll end up reporting myself as dangerously overweight, or look as if I'm lying. Boldly I put down 12 and a half stone, which is a reasonable approximation. There is a list of common ailments and I am asked to indicate simply Y or N to each (except the gynaecological ones, where I put N/A to show I was paying attention). There are one or two tricky ones. For instance, 'Cough'. Well - everyone's had a cough at one time or another. On the other hand, I don't want to make it look as if I've got a chest complaint. But this may be a trick question! What if these things are compiled by highly sophisticated Americans trained in the latest techniques of item construction. This may be part of a lie scale. Oh dear! In the end I put Y and add the note that I had bronchitis once some years ago. To be on the safe side I also admit to some joint pain. To claim *no* health problems or aches and pains may give rise to suspicion.

There are other items that leave me totally stumped. What is my blood pressure? I don't think I have ever known. I begin to realize at this point that I am a medical illiterate as far as my own body goes. No doubt every decent American knows his or her blood pressure, and monitors it frequently. Who knows, but it may be a regular topic of conversation at small dinner parties? I *think* I know roughly what the normal limits are, but dare not invent a value; if I made a mistake it could be even worse than not knowing it. I leave the space blank, but feel this absence is very noticeable indeed.

But things go from bad to worse. 'What was the result of your last rubella titer?' the form demands. I've never had one of these, and have never heard of the damned thing. (Of course I know what rubella is, and can work out what this item probably refers to.) I realize that the main thrust of this section of the inventory is concerned with immunities. This is obvious in the item 'Have you had a BCG?' Now I'm pretty sure that we all had that when we were young, so I put 'Yes' and invent a date to correspond with my early adolescence. The item continues 'Did it go red and swell?' Now I do know that that was the whole point of the exercise, but really can't remember (a) what happened to mine, or (b)which outcome was a 'good thing', if either. Again, a random response may prove a massively dangerous hostage to fortune. I leave it blank.

The form also asks for the date and result of other tests I've never had and never heard of. I leave these blank without a second thought.

The date of my last chest X-ray is easy enough, although it looks disastrously long ago. I am secure about my tetanus, and also put down I had one injection against hepatitis - this was before we went to Mexico (for the ISA) - this against the item 'Have you been vaccinated against hepatitis: how many injections did you have?'

By this time my spirits have sunk very low. I have visions of having to undergo rigorous and protracted cross-questioning about this apparent total failure on my part to check the state of my health and take adequate protective measures. I also fear that any mistake may jeopardise health care and health insurance. Even more worrying, what happens if they say I can't be allowed in the hospital until all my omissions have been rectified? Will I have to spend days and weeks undergoing protracted - maybe expensive - investigations?

Such fears were partly based on my long and complex negotiations in Scotland to do my doctoral research. As part of these proceedings I had to have a smallpox booster and other vaccinations and immunisations as I intended to observe in the dissecting rooms, laboratories and wards. These had been painful, but I had had time to spare and they were provided free at the University health centre. If the MBH were to demand a round of procedures and/or immunisations then my sabbatical could slip away and so could my meagre store of travellers' cheques.

Anyway, having pored over my questionnaire like a small child struggling with a maths worksheet, I venture back into the office, half expecting the young woman to stop me going any further with this inadequate object. She doesn't say anything, other than to tell me I have to go to the Staff Clinic opposite. She does, however, allocate me this magic 'Unit Number', so I feel I have passed one major hurdle, and have broken into the bureaucratic maze.

I go to the Staff Clinic, where yet another smart young woman receptionist tells me to take a seat. An old man in working clothes and with a strong working-class accent is addressing her with embarrassingly effusive thanks. He calls on heaven to praise and bless her, and adds a more secular touch by hoping that her boyfriend will take her someplace nice, 'cos she deserves it. She replies only minimally to his profuse outbursts and avoids eye contact with him.

The receptionist takes my scrap of paper and asks me to take a seat. A rather daunting looking lady, who looks about sixty, comes out from behind the scenes. I cannot tell if she is a doctor or a nurse. There is a young woman waiting too, as well as a middle-aged one. She takes the middle-aged woman's notes from the desk and takes her backstage. Meanwhile the old man has shuffled back, asking if he shouldn't have his blue card. The receptionist seems surprised he wasn't given it, but goes backstage and returns with it, and gives it to him.

The young woman is seen now. She immediately explains that she's got a cold and would like a decongestant. She goes and comes back almost immediately, clutching a bottle of something. The dispensing seemed remarkably off-hand.

I notice a plaque warning sternly that nobody will be seen without their blue addressograph card. I wonder again: have I got one? I don't think so. Should I have one? I don't know. By this time I am reconciled to going with the tide of bureaucracy, and resolved to plead foreignness and ignorance at every turn. While I am waiting the receptionist at the desk says I won't have to wait long, and 'they'll probably just want to check your immunities'.

Shortly after the young woman has received her decongestant the stern, elderly lady emerges, looks at my bits of paper and ushers me into the back regions.

In retrospect what transpired between me and the stern elderly doctor/nurse reads as if I were not only an incompetent outsider to the culture, but also as if I had abandoned all curiosity. I never discovered what status the woman had, what title she bore, precisely what her job was or what power she wielded. As a rabbit can, proverbially, be mesmerised by a snake, I was reduced from a constantly questioning observer into a numbed client, being passively processed. (And as my American colleagues would point out, only a Brit would be such a passive recipient of professional ministrations.)

It transpired that even my half-hearted attempts at the immunities schedule was a failure and its contents - or rather the lack of them - seemed to confirm me as a moral cripple, medically speaking.

The doctor/nurse was surprised and disapproving of my lack of a rubella titer. She commented that this was something she had come across before (in foreigners/Britishers) . She had said to one man "But what if you give rubella to your female patients?" and he'd replied "Well *they're* supposed to get themselves vaccinated." I had the impression that my own failure was bracketed with this man's clear lack of responsibility. In order to remedy my lack of a rubella titer (my moral defects being beyond her) the doctor/nurse took a blood sample. She told me to take off my jacket and asked "Which is your best vein?" I began to wonder if this was something else I was supposed to know. I unbuttoned both cuffs and said "I'll let you decide." "You're supposed to say they are both good," she replied. She decided on my right arm and then addressed me as if I were a child; "Look at the colour television in the corner." (There wasn't one, of course, but presumably the small child is supposed to become preoccupied looking for it.) Stubbornly I watched the blood flow into the phial.

My BCG item also proved troublesome. The doctor/nurse seemed surprised that I had had such a thing muttering that she had not thought it had been done much since the war. I now felt a representative of primitive health care. She assumed that I had had the BCG because I had been exposed to TB and decided that I ought to have a chest X-ray. At about this point in her scrutiny of my deficient moral status she commented, "You have an accent. I'm always very suspicious of anyone with an accent." So my status as an incompetent was enhanced by the 'suspicious' stigma of being a foreigner. The total incompetence which had informed my questionnaire replies was further confirmed when she looked at my answer to the item on hepatitis. Again she asked me to justify what I had written and I explained that I'd had a gammaglobulin injection before visiting Mexico. Crossly she scratched out her note and said "Don't confuse that with vaccination. We do that too for travellers. It isn't vaccination."

This was about the end of my humiliation. I took her offer of a band aid, as my arm was still oozing a little. (I recall now that at various points in this litany of inadequacy I mumbled "Well, I'm not medically qualified", sounding and feeling like a naughty boy making a feeble excuse.)

This completes my medical inspection. I have to wait for the results of my rubella titer, and go and have a chest X-ray as soon as is convenient. For the moment I have to go to yet another office and get my 'Blue Card'. I am directed to a new building, which houses primary care services. I ask for further directions at the information desk and am directed into a modern open-plan office. A number of women are typing away at machines, while members of the public respond to questions and supply information. One of the women finishes with her client, and indicates that I am to come and sit by her. I explain that I have been sent over from the Staff Clinic. She seems indifferent. I go through a new bureaucratic routine, giving her my Boston address (BU again) and the names of my next of kin and my health insurance company. The result of these negotiations is a blue plastic card, the size and format of a credit card. It has my name, my address and my Unit Number. ALWAYS BRING THIS CARD it says. I silently vow to do so. The clerical assistant indicates that the award of this trophy marks the end of our transaction. I thank her and then confuse her. "Excuse me," I say, "Could you tell what I have just done?" She looks puzzled; presumably most people who sit by her VDU and divulge their personal details know what they are doing and why they are doing it. At this stage, however, the full significance of my blue card escapes me. She offers a brief and not very illuminating explanation. I *think* it all means that I am now registered as a potential patient of the hospital. I am a name and a number on their computer.

I return to the Cabot Building and go to Staff Records - getting lost only once on the way, and being rescued by a member of the hospital staff. [Later I shall recognize that all members of staff spend a good deal of time directing perplexed members of the public and other visitors round the labyrinthine muddle of buildings and corridors.] This part of the process goes without a hitch, and I am in time for my appointment with Dr. Peacock.

Summarizing these episodes in a letter home I wrote:

I felt very British and incompetent - I didn't know my blood pressure, for instance!

However, I did become registered at MBH. Eventually I obtained the magic identity card from Security. It was not on the designated Tuesday, however. When I turned up there I discovered that somebody had forgotten to turn on a machine and they weren't taking ID photographs that day. In the end, however, I was able to write home:

> I'm now officially a member of staff at MBH: my ID card says I may be called in in case of a Disaster. I can't imagine what catastrophe could necessitate my presence!

I did occasionally fantasize about using my card to force a way through the crowd to interview the survivors of a major disaster in the tradition of Schatzman and Strauss (1955) or Erikson (1976). To my lasting relief, there was never any such disaster.

At the Mug 'n' Muffin

As I left the MBH after this public revelation of my incompetence as a potential patient and staff member - for how could I lurk among haematologists at the forefront of the field if I didn't know what a rubella titer was? - I felt in need of quiet and refreshment away from the hospital. Accordingly I headed for the local branch of the Mug 'n' Muffin, a cafe that serves coffee and several varieties of muffin (blueberry, bran, corn, apple etc.). The longer I stayed in the United States the more fond I became of blueberry muffins, which of course are nothing like English muffins. The choice of flavours for things like doughnuts, muffins and icecreams is characteristic of American consumerism, and a grave threat to the waistline of the visitor and the native alike.

As I sat at my table, sipping my coffee and nibbling my muffin, I reflected on my manifest incompetence. I had been made to look pretty hopeless, naive and ignorant, I thought. The feeling helped to enhance my general feeling of disorientation and marginality. I had yet to discover whether I would actually be able to collect data of the sort I was hoping for, and my personal circumstances were far from ideal. Boston is expensive, my UK salary was a pittance in dollars, and I was staying in a very uncomfortable room, as I recount later in this paper. I had retired to the Mug 'n' Muffin in the search for a quiet haven to reflect and lick my wounds. For some reason the prospects of chest X-rays always seem alarming to me; I think I suffer from some atavistic fear of consumption. I was genuinely apprehensive of getting involved in protracted medical-cum-bureaucratic hassles over my health status, when all I wanted to do was to observe, and maybe tape record some case conferences and similar encounters. But lay medicine pursued me and my shortcomings were brought home to me again.

The small tables in the cafe were fairly close together, and it was difficult to avoid overhearing nearby conversations. In any case, since I was on my own, a little lonely, and as nosey as ever, I was quite happy to eavesdrop. From time to time I would justify my inquisitiveness by a mute appeal to my 'ethnographic imagination', a general commitment to observation and recording of everyday life. The table nearest mine was occupied by a group of five young people. They looked like students (a vast number of young people in Boston are full-time or part-time students of some sort): they conformed to the style of blue jeans, nylon blousons, trainers or sneakers and small brightly coloured backpacks. They conversed in the loud tones of confident self-absorption.

The theme of their conversation provided a counterpoint to my own recent discomfiture: blood pressure. They talked animatedly about *their* blood pressure. Each of these young people (one boy and four girls) seemed to be able to cite the precise values for recent readings of his or her blood pressure. They appeared to be engaged in a verbal contest of fitness. The precise calibration of blood pressure apparently provided a handy calculus not only of physical well-being, but of personal virtue as well.

The students compared their exercise routines and regimes for effects on blood pressure. One girl told the others that since she had taken up swimming her blood pressure had come down. Another said that she had taken up running, and her blood pressure had come down almost immediately. (How did she know, I wondered? Had she been engaged in an obsessive self-monitoring programme, as well as embarking on exercise? Probably so!)

Not only did these students seem au fait with their own blood pressure, they also seemed familiar with that of their family members too.They discussed members of their respective kindreds who have hypertension. One of the girls recounts the example of her aunt who had been hypertensive. The rest of the family had brought her a dog and her blood pressure had come down dramatically. 'What about the dog's blood pressure?' asked one of the others. I was fascinated by their quick confirmation of all my fears that ignorance of one's own state of health marked me out as an alien - probably from an underdeveloped country. Perhaps, I wondered, blood pressure is one of the things one has to know about (like the Constitution, I suppose) in order to become a naturalized American citizen. Clearly I would fail. My morale had sunk even lower, despite the therapeutic effects of the blueberry muffin and my first mug of coffee.

Later when I tried to share the 'blood pressure' part of my initiation into the MBH with American friends their reactions confirmed my status as outsider and incompetent. They agreed, sympathetically, that to ask me for my blood pressure was unreasonable because - after all - I had just flown the Atlantic so it would not be at its normal value, rendering the data worthless. Collapse of stout medical sociologist.

While I was getting my first top-up of coffee the young people left, still chattering loudly. I briefly resented their self-assurance and then turned to inspect some of the other customers. One pair in particular caught my attention. They looked for all the world like a couple of characters out of Damon Runyon. In my imagination the Mug 'n' Muffin in Boston was transformed into Mindy's on Broadway. One old guy was doing most of the talking.

He was wearing an open-necked shirt, with baggy brown trousers, topped off by a scruffy overcoat. He had wispy white hair and held a rolled newspaper. To begin with this latter was wagged for emphasis; later it was thrust into the overcoat pocket. His companion was more striking. His greying fair hair was cropped in a severe crew cut. He wore a bright blue jacket with a loud design of large checks. His accessories included a slightly wilting gardenia in his button hole, a bow tie, and a much chewed small cigar, which he kept clamped between his teeth.

Luckily this intriguing looking pair were just within earshot and I tuned in as best I could, expecting to escape from my medical preoccupations. What would be their topic of conversation? What animated the talker and kept the attention of his listener? The dismal showing of the Red Sox, maybe, or the prospects for the Celtics? Perhaps they were reliving the joy felt in Greater Boston the previous winter when a senior at Boston College, Doug Flutie (nicknamed 'Flutie the Cutie' or 'The Magic Flutie') had played so well BC had reached an important inter-varsity football final. Better still if their talk would take me into the world of Scott's (1968) *The Racing Game*, in which men play the ponies, and compare the louse book with the organized book or swap stories of horse rooms they have known and sure things which mysteriously failed to win. . Boston is a great city for sports fans and I expected sports talk. Instead it was immediately apparent that the subject of their shared interest was medicine. Not blood pressure to begin with, but medical malpractice. The 'expert' was regaling his companion with stories not of slow horses but medical mistakes. He recounted a tale of a man who had received a transfusion of blood from the wrong group. This patient had, he told the wide-eyed listener, died in twenty-six seconds. The narrator recounts his tale with an air of authority and goes on to display more and more of his medical 'expertise' (the source of which never becomes apparent). The next topic which I could overhear turned out to be even more startling. The narrator took a paper napkin and accompanied the account with a diagram: ...'and then they put the speculum right up the lady's vagina, and so they can see what's going on...' His friend was clearly impressed. 'Oh, hey, I never could figure that out,' he acknowledged.

Continuing the gynaecological/obstetrical theme, our expert then went on to elaborate on the developmental stages of the embryo (pronounced to rhyme with Ohio). For the most part these details were recounted in a loud voice, but from time to time their heads came closer together and the volume was reduced to that of normal conversation only (and hence inaudible from my table). When the conversation resumed transmission in my direction the topic had changed again. Now our 'expert' was laying down the law on the colour of the patient's stools in various medical conditions. But he went on to warn his friend not to confuse that with the effect of iron tablets, which can also blacken the stool. His friend looked suitably impressed with this intelligence, and seemed fortified against any future misinterpretation of that sort. He mumbled appreciation and encouragement while his companion pursued his synopsis of medical knowledge. He touched lightly on the alcohol content of patent tonics and soporifics, and they began to talk about the consequences of drinking. The expert told his friend about cirrhosis, regaling him with a graphic description of the liver in the last stages of the disease. They continued to converse in audible tones, engrossed in their lay medical gossip: the one in imparting it, the other in eliciting and receiving it.

Finally, their coffee finished and their conversation at an end. They prepared to leave and as they collected the bill from the waitress, the one in the blue jacket confided to his friend, 'I've never told you this before, but I'll tell you now, I only associate with respectable people'. To which he replied 'Well, I tell yer, you'll learn a lot from me.' So, well satisfied with each other's company, they left.

Soon after the two gentlemen had vacated their table it was taken by two elderly ladies - of highly respectable appearance. One immediately started to tell her friend about somebody who had 'been in a week', having had a heart attack. She then went on to describe her own foot and leg, and how well she was now walking.

I found I'd had quite enough of lay medicine and gave up trying to monitor the conversation. Entertained, but not as reassured as I might have hoped, I too paid and left, plunging onto the T at Park Station and returning to Longwood on the Green Line. I scribbled my notes as best I could in my lonely little room late into the night.

True confessions or self-conscious anti-heroics?

The twenty years since Hammond's *Sociologists at Work* (1964) have seen a number of similar 'confessional' volumes by sociologists. Britain has produced collections edited by Bell and Newby (1977), Bell and Roberts (1984), Burgess (1984). There is the Australian compilation edited by Bell and Encel (1978). From the United States the confessional mode includes such recent volumes as Jacobs (1970) Messerschmidt (1981) None of these has achieved the sales and publicity of equivalent volumes by anthropologists confessing their naiveties in the foreign field. Bowen's *Return to Laughter* (1954) was a bestseller for book clubs such as the Readers Union, and most recently Nigel Barley's (1983) has been read far beyond academic anthropological circles. The best known literary approximation of this genre is Alison Lurie's fictional account of fieldwork, *Imaginary Friends* (1978).

These accounts are all, in various degrees, characterized by an ambivalence towards the author/narrator. As a matter of good research practice we all enjoin a reflexive self-awareness on the part of the ethnographer, as a methodological imperative of interpretative social science (Hammersley and Atkinson, 1983). But the content of these autobiographical accounts goes beyond the recounting of methods, data collection, and interpretation. They are replete with *moral* evaluations of the author/fieldworker. There is a constant tension between the imagery of the ethnographer as moral hero, and the ethnographer as anti-hero. We know that methodologists like John Lofland tell us to behave like a 'socially acceptable incompetent' (Lofland 1971). Sometimes in our reflexive autobiographical accounts we stress the dimension of social acceptability, sometimes we explore and confess our incompetence. Something of the ambivalence is caught in the following extracts from an autobiographical account I wrote.

> Boston is not a bad place to immerse yourself in medical work and medical knowledge. It is richly endowed with hospitals and medical schools. In the past and in the present it is second to none as a medical metropolis. As in most of the institutions of Boston and nearby Cambridge, the most modern facilities stand cheek by jowl with reminders of the Colonial days and of more recent history. Certainly I was thoroughly submerged in a medical ambience. Having arrived in Boston to undertake fieldwork in a medical setting I even found myself living in a hospital (or at least the annexe of one). The pound was tumbling against the dollar. (It has since been accepted by my colleagues in Economics that any intention on my part to visit the United States is guaranteed to push the pound sharply down. Plans to cross the Atlantic seem to constitute a self-defeating prophecy.) I had found a room at about half the standard rent in a hostel attached to the Children's Hospital. The lower floors of the building housed administrative and research offices for the hospital. The sixth floor consisted of rooms for visiting parents of children in the hospital. The top floor contained tiny garrets for a small number of students and other lowly forms of life (such as ethnographers).
>
> The accommodation was, to say the least, spartan. The only floor covering was a layer of fluff and grit. The bed was metal framed and sprung, with a knobbly mattress and one incredibly thin blanket. A grubby handbasin and a tiny desk were the other notable features. The room measured about nine feet by six feet. One of the most depressing things was the fact that my personal belongings fitted into this small cell with room to spare. I never managed the temperature of that room. It was heated with an old-fashioned radiator; on most days it threw out a heat so fierce

that it was unbearable to touch it for long enough even to turn it down or off. (The aged controls were unpredictable in their effect anyway.) Since we were enjoying an Indian summer the room became unbearably hot by day. The only way of regulating the temperature was by opening the window, itself a hazardous undertaking. Sleep was only possible with one's feet roasting and one's head caressed by a chilly draught (or vice versa). I hated that radiator: it clanked unpredictably and malevolently. A companion to it in one of the lavatories inflicted severe burns down one leg when I stumbled against it; I looked as if I had been barbecue grilled. My view was of a rooftop car park. In his autobiographical account of his first year at the Harvard Medical School, *Gentle Vengeance* Le Baron (1982) described life in the quadrangle and hall of residence just round the corner from where I was living. He says that in the distance he could see the illuminated sign for the Citgo oil company at Kenmore Square. Trapped as he was in the unremitting grind of medical school, that sign in the sky became an icon of escape to the real world of the city. I could see it in the middle distance too. While I was not as restricted as the medical students the Citgo sign was also for me a symbol of socially distant everyday life as I ground out my fieldnotes in wretched seclusion.

It was an odd place for a medical sociologist to be living - more or less in a hospital. Not just one hospital, indeed. The Children's Hospital in Boston is but one part of a huge medical complex in the 'Longwood' area. Sandwiched between the poor black area of Roxbury to the south and the affluent suburb of Brookline (described evocatively in Lightfoot, 1983) to the north, Longwood consists almost entirely of hospitals and clinics. Standing in very close proximity are the Beth Israel Hospital, The Childrens', the Brigham and Women's, the Deaconess, the Massachusetts Mental Health Center, the Dana-Faber Institute, and others. Last, but by no means least, the Harvard Medical School nestles amidst it all. It is an odd place to be living. Apart from hospitals there is remarkably little in the way of everyday life. At night there is nothing stirring but ambulances; occasional medical, nursing and other hospital personnel; and - most noticeable to an outsider - armed security guards. As a would-be fieldworker it was rather like living above the shop. I would lie in bed sometimes when I first arrived and wonder just what might be going on in all the wards, laboratories, nurses' stations and corridors. A more serious and immediate personal problem was that the area contained little or nothing in the way of shops or diners, so food had to be obtained elsewhere. My lifeline was a van, parked outside the hospital twenty four hours a day that sold things like kebabs and pitta bread, doughnuts and coffee.

Actually these privations added a rather romantic touch to my field trip. It was possible to redefine my Spartan surroundings and see myself in an heroic light. My bare little room became in fantasy the garret of bohemian and romantic mythology. The inevitably lonely and demanding experience of fieldwork in a strange setting could be transformed into a personal narrative of quest and survival. I was living proof that it is not only the archetypical anthropologist in an 'exotic' milieu who can suffer physical privation and existential Angst and disorientation.

It was an odd experience for me - working as a medical sociologist - to be living (however uncomfortably) in the midst of a vast complex of hospitals. At night the area was all but deserted, by day it was thronged with people. Even more odd, perhaps, was the fact that I was not doing my fieldwork in any of the hospitals in the neighbourhood. Mine was one of the major teaching hospitals elsewhere in the city. On the other hand, uncomfortable as it was, my accomodation provided rather useful in a symbolic sense. My cramped, underfurnished, scruffy (none too clean) room was a surrogate artist's garret. We are accustomed to romantic images of the solitary writer or artist struggling with his (almost always his) art. The solititude and the privation combine to provide the right scenario for the romantic hero. Despite the mudane nature of much of my work, therefore, the attic room and its spartan atmosphere helped to construct a suitable backdrop for the mock-epic of my fieldwork experience.

Conclusion

The question that I want to raise through this chapter, then, is this: Why do we (ethnographers in general) so often produce autobiographical accounts of this sort? Susan Sontag (1966) has written on the anthropologist as 'hero'. Just as often the anthropologist or sociologist seem to present him or herself in an anti-heroic light. In effect the resulting self-presentation is an ambivalent mixture of the two. There is the wry tradition whereby we rehearse the second-worst thing that ever happened to us in the field, the very worst being too painful or embarrassing). We paint ourselves in unflattering colours: we are by turns naive, vulnerable and incompetent. Of course, we are meant to present ourselves as 'socially acceptable incompetents' for the purposes of data collection. Yet it appears that we are often genuinely incompetent - lacking street wisdom and credibility: 'the sociologist as schlemiel' is a long-running thread in the genre. By the same token, our struggles with an unfamiliar, even hostile, social environment can invest this character with more praiseworthy qualities. Of course, the standard sociologist working in his or her own culture can hardly compete with the average social anthropologist. Our research settings are just not that exotic for the most part. Even medical sociologists do not normally run the risk of contracting obscure tropical diseases. Our privations and dangers (physical and moral) are not as extreme. The food in the average hospital staff canteen may be grim (it is), but does not compete with wierd and wonderful cuisines endured by 'proper' anthropologists. Perhaps the ethnographer like myself - especially one with a kosher training as an anthropologist - has an inferiority complex. 'Look', our accounts say, 'I've had to suffer too; you just can't begin to understand all I had to get through to get those data.' We offset the manifest arrogance and exploitation of social investigation by self-deprecation. The anti-hero, or even the clown, is valuable camouflage. The result is a highly ambiguous 'trickster' figure, inscribed in these artful autobiographical revelations. Our mirror of 'true confessions' is equally a mask of self-regard. I have suggested in the compoanion chapter to this one that the revelations of ethnographic confessions cannot be regarded as the unmediate, unvarnished truth any more than realist ethnographic accopunts can. Confessions are guided by conventions and expectations, just like any other genre of text. We portray ourselves between the heroic and the pathetic in order to achieve certain conventional effects, I suggest. We do not write and read sociological or anthropological confessions in order to improve the quality of epistemology or the practice of research methods in the field. Nor do we do it solely in order to debunk and amuse. The texts might well realise both those functions, of course. The genre of the confessional captures the tension between innocence and knowing, between purpose and circumstance, so that our cultural understanding and our academic street-credibility can be displayed as hard-won trophies. We can express our own struggles, and vicariously experience the struggles of others, in appreciating what achievements they are. Equally, however, the cultural requirements of due modesty are observed through self-portrayals as mildly bumbling and incompetent characters. The autobiographical account thus pays our dues and reflects various deep-seated values. We can celebrate our esoteric knowledge and the unique experience of our own research while appearing to engage in due modesty through self-deprecation and self-mockery.

In the previous chapter I dissected a limited corpus of urban confessions taken from the self-revelations of sociologists or anthropologists writing in a particular genre. In this chapter I have contributed a rather similar kind of text myself. In constructing it I did not work back from my embryonic formal analysis in order to try to make a canonical text of my own. The chronological order of composition was in fact the reverse of that. I had drafted this chapter before I began to write and present the substance of my reflections on urban confessions. It was, rather, the experience of writing yet another confessional for yet another collection of them (McKeganey and Cunningham-Burley 1988) that started me thinking about the genre in more general terms.

We saw in the previous chapter that sociologists and anthropologists frequently portray themselves in ambivalent ways: as hero and as schlemiel.

This is often couched in a tone of arch self-mockery. This chapter obviously displays the latter tendency. It is essentially an anti-heroic self-presentation in which the sociologist-as-anti-hero recounts his own ineptitude. Such an account simultaneously plays down the ethnographer's personal attributes, while celebrating his or her cpacity for reflective insight. The anti-hero may thus solicit the sympathetic identification of the reader, who is invited to enjoy a Woody Allen-like self portrait (full of bewildered self-deprecation). This stands in sharp contrast to the more common heroic stereotype of the intrepid explorer, or even of the anthropologist. The urban sociologist, or the sociological investigator of organizational settings, cannot always lay claim to the kind of physical and moral danger implied in more exotic expeditions. The settings of research, the 'field', are so much more often domesticated and familiar. We have seen that some authors, like Wolf, can look back on moments of physical threat, and research on crime and deviance is often able to evoke more colourful images of danger and heroism. The ethnographer under fire is able to display an adequate degree of cool composure.

By contrast, the ordinary ethnographer of the mundane must eke out whatever effects are going. On the one hand, the shreds of the heroic can be eked out, with every difficulty and deprivation milked for all it is worth. The reader's sympathy can be evoked, and the research process portrayed as a noble, and ennobling, struggle. On the other hand, the elevated aspects of the narrative provide a backdrop for the more bathetic elements of the tale. If we cannot be thoroughly heroic, then we can always try to evoke wry sympathy and humour. In so doing, of course, we continually emphasise the personal and moral vicissitudes that we must go through in order to complete our work in the field. Our knowledge is hard won. So too, we tell our readers, is the self-knowledge and the wisdom that allows us to reflect on our experiences and narrate them with such apparent (but artful) candour.

7 · Goffman's poetics

Introduction

Goffman was a *stylist*. His writing had a very characteristic voice. Commentators sometimes find it difficult to transcend Goffman's style; either one descends to pale imitation and pastiche, or one's own text seems leaden and pedestrian by comparison. Berman (1972) enters some very strong claims concerning Goffman's writing, suggesting that he was outstandingly able to convey the conditions of everyday life in contemporary society. The early works in particular established Goffman as a unique author within the sociological canon. Manning (1976) was among the first commentators to remark on the special role of literary form and style in Goffman's *oeuvre*, suggesting that his method was grounded in his use of literary conventions such as metaphor. Goffman defied categorization in relation to a particular school or tradition of sociological theory. Moreover, he rarely wasted his creative energies on debating and defending his work vis-a-vis other scholars and critics. He drew on other authors, of course, but never in a spirit of pedantry or polemic: if anything, perhaps, his use of other sources was cavalier. Williams (1983:99) draws attention to this and mentions one of the very rare occasions on which Goffman acted out of character, as it were.

> His unwillingness to locate himself within any particular theoretical tradition was indirectly shown in his idiosyncratic style of referencing throughout his work, though the most direct statement on this issue came in a carefully irascible reply (Goffman 1981) to an assessment of *Frame Analysis* by Norman Denzin and Charles Keller (1981). Quite apart from his dissatisfaction with their understanding and description of the details of that particular book, two additional characteristics of the essay earned his special disapprobation. First, their tendency to treat his work as a substantive whole, a collection of studies

structured so as to constitute a unity of effort, able to be characterised by some algorithm, reference to which would permit an understanding of work accomplished and prediction of work yet to come. Second, their desire to locate his work within some definable 'tradition', 'school' or 'paradigm', the more easily to evaluate the nature of its contribution to modern sociology. Both of these tendencies he saw to be more regrettable, representing to him a colourless pedagogical interest in the discipline rather than a lively engagement with its practice and products.

Any essay such as this will inevitably risk equivalent strictures on Goffman's behalf. It will, however, attempt to remain faithful to something of Goffman's spirit.

One of the commonplace observations to be made about Goffman's texts is that their persuasive power (if any) does not usually rest on conventional canons of scholarly self-presentation. We the readers are not offered the normal justificatory apparatus of, say, 'methods' and a corpus of specially marked 'data'. Even those essays which draw most closely on Goffman's 'fieldwork' make little in the way of concessions to the conventions of 'ethnographic' reportage. Of other data sources even Goffman is conventionally given to disclaimers. For instance, in *Relations in Public* (Goffman 1972) he writes of his method and his data:

> Throughout the papers in this volume unsubstantiated assertions are made regarding the occurrence of certain social practices in certain times and among peoples of various kinds. This description by pronouncement is claimed to be a necessary evil... (p.18)

And

> Certainly ... the method that often is resorted to here - unsystematic, naturalistic observation - has very serious limitations.... (p.20).

While in the introductory section of *Frame Analysis* he writes:

> There are lots of good grounds for doubting the kind of analysis about to be presented. I would do so myself if it weren't my own. It is too bookish, too general, too removed from fieldwork to have a good chance of being anything more than another mentalistic adumbration. (p.13)

Despite Goffman's somewhat cavalier approach to method, the

heterogeneous and heterodox nature of his source-material, his reluctance to 'locate' his own work in broader sociological contexts ('never explain, never apologise' seems to have been the watchword), his work has achieved quite extraordinarily wide audiences. His appeal seems to rest not on the usual criteria of 'good' sociology or social psychology. Indeed, as Fine and Martin (1995) remark, the empirical basis of his work does not stand up to any of the normal crieria for sound sociological research. The empirical basis of, say, *Asylums* is difficult to assess, because of Goffman's inadequate methodological discussions, and does not compare with the best ethnographies of organizations or medical settings. Rather, his appeal to his readers, and his stature as a sociologist, derive from the distinctive, not to say unique, persuasive style of his writing. Perhaps more than any other modern sociologist, Goffman's analysis was *rhetorical*. Writing of *Asylums* Fine and Martin suggest that:

> In sum, despite Goffman's status as one of the most important American sociologists of the twentieth century, he is not among the century's best ethnographers. His ethnography is casual, not methodologically thorough, and perhaps not to be trusted in providing a precise picture of this social institution. Ultimately, Goffman wishes to provide a perspective, not a photograph. For a 'fair' reading of life in an institution, other ethnographies must be relied upon. In the theory and in the *presentation* of the theory we find the glories of Goffman the 'ethnographer'. (emphasis in original)

Fine and Martin go on to discuss the particular tropes of humour in Goffman's work, especially in *Asylums*: sarcasm, satire and irony. They are perhaps characteristic of yet a more general tone in Goffmans distinctive voice: the exhortatory tone of the *moralist*.

Goffman's work resists translation into an overarching set of theoretical precepts or propositions. This applies not only to his *oeuvre* taken as a whole but to each work. There are, of course, themes and threads which run through the works, which are developed and elaborated in them:

> Throughout his 25 years of published work he did develop and consolidate a stable core of basic concepts for the analysis of social interaction, and it was a core with a highly integrated hierarchical structure of interlocking definitions and usages. It ranged from the description of the overall structuring context of interaction defined by the concept 'occasion', through to the most basic unit of his collection, that of 'move', defined as 'everything conveyed by an actor during a turn at taking action'. (Williams, 1983, pp.100-101)

Williams goes on to note, in a way especially pertinent to this paper, that this 'core' was constantly elaborated on and overlaid:

> Yet that core was continually being worked at, modified and developed by Goffman, until it was surrounded by more and more laminations in his text, and it is at this level that many readers find his writing troublesome, over-literary and speculative. (p.101)

This 'literary' quality is of course so thoroughly well known that in itself it requires no elaboration. John Lofland's essay on the topic notes in relation to Goffman's early work:

> The material offered by Goffman is somewhat new, but it is not as startling as some of his readers seem to believe. The fascination with Goffman rests, rather, upon the peculiar way he goes about his work rather than on the mere naked content of what he is saying. (Lofland, 1980, p.24)

Lofland identifies a number of features of Goffman's style, which will be referred to later in this essay. Manning, too, draws attention to the centrality of style in the context of his essay on Goffman's later works. Others too have commented on the rhetorical nature of Chicago-school and cognate sociologies.

There is, then, consensus about the importance of Goffman's written style. Likewise, commentators are in general agreement about the salient features of it. They agree that the persuasive and pleasing force of Goffman's texts derives from his use of *metaphor* and *irony* or *perspective by incongruity*. They document and exemplify rhetorical devices of these sorts in illustrating the distinctive quality of Goffman's writing.

Now the purpose of this essay is not to dispute these earlier contributions. On the contrary: the insights of previous authors will quite unashamedly be incorporated in built upon. Rather I want to suggest that there is room for a more detailed and fine-grained consideration of Goffman's textuality, and further, that we can develop a more systematic parallel between Goffman's style and the substance of his sociology. As with so many aspects of Goffman and commentary on him, it is difficult to claim any great measure of originality for oneself. My own attempt is fraught with its own irony: the more one attempts to concentrate on the *detail* of the texts, the more difficult it becomes to do justice to the range of the work.

I want to begin that analysis with the following quotation:

> He often enters the field of inquiry from any point whatsoever, without any apparent importance; he discovers an insight here, another there, as he finds them and turns to a third. He soon has

a multitude in each hand, rejects something in order to exchange it for something that came before, strikes some more blows with his spade, uncovers new insights and suddenly finds that he has turned up all the ground around him and is buried waist-deep, and digs until he reaches the botom. It is always a renewed pleasure to experience this with him.

Now that is not a description of Goffman, nor indeed of any sociologist. Written by Muschg, and cited by Roustang (1983), it is in fact a characterization of the style of Sigmund Freud. I cite it at the outset not to propose that Freud's style and Goffman's are identical, but that our understanding of both authors is particularly dependent upon an appreciation of their style, or the *poetics* of their writen texts.

Roustang's reflections on Freud - especially in relation to the interpretation of dreams - suggest that there is a direct correspondence, or homology, between the analytic *method* and the style of its textual realization. Roustang proposes that Freud's style is marked by a heavy reliance on *parataxis*. That is, 'the place given to words in a sentence, or in a series of sentences, independent of the liaisons furnished by the prepositions, conjunctions, declensions and conjugations necessary to syntax' (Roustang, 1983, p.17). The style is not devoid of syntax, of course: otherwise it would be unintelligible. The point is, rather, that Freud's argument is not represented through propositional forms that are in turn dependent on syntactic elaboration. In Roustang's own words:

> Freud's use of parataxis is not fortuitous. If his style is marked by it, it is because he must bring to the forefront what is characteristic of infantilism, the archaic, and the psychoneuroses. Freud gives us a genuine definition of parataxis in a passage from his *New Introductory Lectures* dealing with dreams: 'All the linguistic means by which the finer relations of thoughts are expressed, the conjunctions and prepositions, the changes of declension and conjugation, escape, because there are no means of expression for it; as in a primitive language without grammar, only the raw material of thought is expressed, the abstract returns to the concrete on which it is based.' Freud perhaps ignored that in writing on the dream whose energy derives from infantile sources, in showing the link between the dream and the psychoneuroses, in trying to discover there 'some primaeval relic of humanity', his style underwent, through all the subtleties of syntax and through their omission, a paratactic regression. (p. 17)

In other words, Roustang is arguing here, there is a direct homology between the style and the subject-matter of Freud's intepretation of dreams.

98

We shall return to some of the specific stylistic devices identified by Roustang subsequently. There is no need to claim an identity between Goffman and Freud in order to learn from Roustang's insights. I shall argue that, like Freud, Goffman relies upon a number of 'paratactic' features, and that many aspects of Goffman's texts are those of Freud's also. The reasons for such stylistic similarity again derive not from an identity of substantive or theoretical interest. Rather, they reflect the parallelism in their methodology and the textual representation of their semiotics.

Classic texts

It is clearly not possible to undertake an exhaustive analysis of the texts of an author as prolific as Goffman. On the contrary, only the most sketchy of exemplifications is possible. Some limits to the task have been established at the outset. For the purposes of this paper, only the earlier corpus of works has been sampled (e.g. *The Presentation of Self in Everyday Life*; *Stigma*; *Relations in Public*, *Asylums* etc.). Within that corpus a mixture of random and purposive sampling has been employed. It must be emphasized, however, that only the most fragmentary of analyses is attempted in a preliminary and exploratory fashion. Arguably this approach is in keeping with Goffman's analytic spirit.

Without further justification I shall begin with an introductory section taken from the first substantive chapter of *The Presentation of Self*. I shall present an outline analysis of the first four paragraphs of that chapter, on 'Performances'. Each paragraph is reproduced below, with each separate sentence numbered for ease of reference:

> (1) When an individual plays a part he implicitly requests his observers to take seriously the impression that is fostered before them. (2) They are asked to believe that the character they see actually possesses the attributes he appears to possess, that the task he performs will have the consequences that are implicitly claimed for it, and that, in general, matters are what they appear to be. (3) In line with this, there is the popular view that the individual offers his performance and puts on his show 'for the benefit of other people'. (4) It will be convenient to begin a consideration of performances by turning the question around and looking at the individual's own belief in the impression of reality that he attempts to engender in those among whom he finds himself.
>
> (5) At one extreme, one finds that the perfomer can be fully taken in by his own act; he can be sincerely convinced that the impression of reality which he stages is the real reality. (6) When his audience is also convinced in this way about the show he puts on - and this seems to be the typical case - then for the moment

at least, only the sociologist or the socially disgruntled will have any doubts about the 'realness' of what is presented.

(7) At the other extreme, we find that the performer may not be taken in at all by his own routine. (8) This possibility is understandable, since no one is in quite as good an observational position to see through the act as the person who puts it on. (9) Coupled with this, the performer may be moved to guide the conviction of his audience only as a means to other ends, having no ultimate concern in the conception that they have of him or of the situation. (10) When the individual has no belief in his own act and no ultimate concern with the beliefs of his audience, we may call him cynical, reserving the term 'sincere' for individuals who believe in the impression fostered by their own performance. (11) It should be understood that the cynic, with all his professional disinvolvement, may obtain unprofessional pleasures from his masquerade, experiencing a kind of gleeful spiritual aggression from the fact that he can toy at will with something his audience must take seriously.

(12) It is not assumed, of course, that all cynical performers are interested in deluding their audiences for purposes of what is called 'self-interest' or private gain. (13) A cynical individual may delude his audience for what he considers to be their own good, or for the good of the community, etc. (14) For illustrations of this we need no appeal to sadly enlightened showmen such as Marcus Aurelius or Hsun Tzu. (15) We know that in service occupations practitioners who may otherwise be sincere are sometimes forced to delude their customers because their customers show such a heartfelt demand for it. (16) Doctors who are led into giving placebos, filling station attendants who resignedly check and recheck tire pressures for anxious women motorists, shoe clerks who sell a shoe that fits but tell the customer it is the size she wants to hear - these are cynical performers whose audiences will not allow them to be sincere. (17) Similarly, it seems that sympathetic patients in mental wards will sometimes feign bizarre symptoms so that student nurses will not be subjected to a disappointingly sane performance. (18) So also, when inferiors extend their most lavish reception for visiting superiors, the selfish desire to win favor may not be the chief motive; the inferior may be tactfully attempting to put the superior at ease by simulating the kind of world the superior is thought to take for granted.

These introductory paragraphs are tightly ordered and internally coherent. In various ways they are characteristic of many aspects of Goffman's textual style in general. To begin with, the style is *repetitive*. This can be seen at the level of lexical items. The first three paragraphs comprise a group, while the fourth establishes a somewhat different tack, introducing examples more explicitly. If we take just the first three, then, we find a high degree of repetition within and between the paragraphs. It is, of course, hardly surprising that key terms in an analysis should recur, but the density of the interconnections seems quite striking here, and is symptomatic of more general textual features.

The following lexical items are, for example, repeated within the first paragraph: *individual, implicitly, impression, performance, possess, appear*. The following items are repeated between Paragraph 1 and Paragraph 2: *impression, perform(ance/er), reality* (also echoed by *real* and *realness* within Paragraph 2), *show, believe/belief*. The following items are repeated between Paragraph 2 and Paragraph 3: *extreme, perform(ance/er), act, impression, audience, find, taken in, puts on, convince/conviction, sincere(ly)*. If we add items from Paragraph 1 which are repeated in Paragraph 3 but not in 2, then we have the following extra items: *believe, belief, seriously, see*.

In themselves these observations are not very illuminating, of course, and we shall have to show something a bit more systematic if a satisfying characterisation of Goffman (or indeed of any writer) should be attempted. If, however, we stay with this opening group of three paragraphs, then some further variations of paratactic arrangement can be discerned. First, there is the direct echo of the first sentence of paragraph 2 (no.5: 'At one extreme, one finds that the performer may be taken in ...' and the first sentence of paragraph 3 (no. 7: 'At the other extreme, we find that the perfomer may not be taken in...'). This is of course based not simply upon repetition, but also on antithesis, and this too is a recurrent feature of the three paragraphs. Again, even if we single out just words and phrases, then the following antitheses are readily apparent: sincere/ cynical; professional/ unprofessional; means/ends; toy with/seriously.

There is, too, another device whereby paratactic organization is cemented. That is, the device whereby items which occur towards the end of a paragraph are picked up, echoed and used to introduce the next. Note how the important phrase 'impression of reality' is introduced towards the end of the first paragraph. This is then re-stated as the main topic of the opening of the next paragraph. This is observable in the link between Paragraphs 3 and 4, in the repetition of cynic etc. into the 'cynical performer', a type which is then elaborated upon in the fourth paragraph. The rhetorical force of juxtaposition is emphasised through the accumulation of somewhat recondite terms: the notion of 'gleeful spritual aggression' is a striking example in this particular context.

Overall, therefore, these first three of four paragraphs are marked by a high degree of internal cross-linkage and interconnectedness. What is, perhaps, noticeable is the degree to which the argument is introduced and progresses via these repetitious, anaphoric links. The theme of 'performances' is not stated explicitly. It is not defined. The voice of the author is that of an apodeictic impresario. At the outset the sociologist makes only a tentative, quirky sort of appearance - as a potential disbeliever in company with the 'socially disgruntled'. On other occasions in this text the author's voice is submerged in a sort of everyman 'we' who observe and know. It is essentially a voice which is in the text. There is no radical distinction between the 'audience' to the performances described, the wider audience of readers and the sociological observer. Goffman's authorial voice is not there to establish a hierarchy of authenticity any more than there is a hierarchy of conceptual or rhetorical levels.

We must conclude this brief consideration - a starting point in Goffman used as a starting point for this analysis - by turning to the fourth paragraph. It is just as 'typically' Goffmanesque as the previous three. It clearly follows on from the first three but displays a characteristic shift. Here we encounter a massively familiar feature of Goffman's texts - the concatenation of exemplars, drawn both from published sources and common knowledge. This aspect of Goffman's text does not require as great deal of descriptive elaboration here. It is too familiar. Nonetheless it deserves some attention, for it further elaborates our understanding of Goffman's paratactic poetics. Here we encounter that famous stylistic quirk whereby example is strung together with example to construct a kaleidoscope of types and sub-types. At times, perhaps, they may appear to be plucked out and arranged in a happenstance manner. Goffman often appears to present his exemplars as if they were *objets trouves*; and in one sense they are, culled from the academic literature and more popular sources. Goffman is, in that sense, the sociological *bricoleur par excellence*. In our paragraph four, as elsewhere, the exemplars are far from a mere string of more or less apposite illustrations. Goffman's style plays off the internal linkages and oppositions implied in such a list.

The exemplification is introduced with an arrestingly tangential remark: 'For illustrations of this we need not appeal to sadly enlightened showmen such as Marcus Aurelius or Hsun Tzu'. The description of these two luminaries as 'showmen' is itself a striking juxtaposition of items: the rhetorical form of a sort of *oxymoron*. This latter is most characteristic of Goffman's voice. It suffuses the texts' rhetorical forms and is coterminous with its 'moral' tone. In a more general sense it is an ironic tone. Goffman is one of the great exponents of sociological irony.

At the micro-level - the level at which I am working here - we can see the play of recondite juxtaposition in paragraph 4 of 'Performances'. The examples drawn from 'service occupations' show a pleasing diversity and symmetry. Goffman gives us a list in four parts: doctors and their patients, filling station attendants and their clients, shoe clerks and their customers, mental patients and their nurses. The list itself displays the figure of *chiasmus*, of the general form A B B A. That is, in terms of the occupational types - Health Profession, Service Occupation, Service Occupation, Health

Profession. In other words, the juxtaposition of 'caring' professional with fawning and manipulative workers in low-status occupations is reinforced by its immediate repetition in inverted order. The symmetry is not perfect, however, for the chiasmus itself incorporates a further inversion, between the two 'medical' examples. In the first doctors deceive their patients, in the latter the patients dupe the professionals. In both cases, the manipulation of reality serves a more general good. The examples are by no means randomly selected and arranged, therefore. The tone of the passage in question is profoundly ironic, and this is sustained through the juxtapositions and inversions which structure the text.

The paragraph ends with yet another juxtaposition, of inferiors and superiors. Here too we find the theme of inversion carried through. Here the appearance of fawning and currying favour is reinterpreted as a possible reality of tact.The text thus constantly shuttles between appearance and reality, between strangely assorted categories of persons, or between antithetical pairings.

If we return for a moment to Roustang's commentary on Freud, then we find very much the same range of textual features being identified in the 'interpretation of dreams'.. Roustang comments on the extent to which the repetition of key words is used to impart coherence to and and advance the text. In a way very similar to one of Goffman's practices, 'Freud constantly uses (the) classical procedure of concatentation, in which the words of the preceding paragraph are repeated at the beginning of the following one.' (Roustang, p.9) Remember in relation to our passage from 'Performances' how the term 'cynic' is introduced towards the end of paragraph 3, and becomes the key term at the outset of paragraph 4.

Likewise, the use of *chiasmus*, and *inclusion* is found in the key passages from Freud. Roustang identifies one paragraph which includes the following pattern of repetition and inversion of terms: *aimless and arbitrary*; *dream-thoughts*; *dream-thoughts*; *arbitrary and witty*. The figure of inclusion comprises the repetition of words and phrases at the beginning and end of a paragraph. The embedding of a further repetition, as here, and as in the Goffman list reproduced above, generates chiasmus.

Let us continue the analysis with reference to another fragment - this time from 'Normal Appearances', in *Relations in Public*:

(1) Individuals, whether in human or animal form, exhibit two basic modes of activity. (2) They go about their business grazing, gazing, mothering, digesting, building, resting, playing, placidly attending to easily managed matters at hand. (3) Or, fully mobilized, a fury of intent, alarmed, they get ready to attack or to stalk or to flee. (4) Physiology itself is patterned to coincide with this duality.

(5) The individual mediates between these two tendencies with a very pretty capacity for dissociated vigilance. (6) Smells,

sounds, sights, touches, pressures - in various combinations, depending on the species - provide a running reading of the situation, a constant monitoring of what surrounds. (7) But by a wonder of adaptation these readings can be done out of the furthest corner of whatever is serving for an eye, leaving the individual himself free to focus his main attention on the non-emergencies around him. (8) Matters that the actor has become accustomed to will receive a flick or a shadow of concern, one that decays as soon as he obtains a microsecond of confirmation that everything is in order; should something really prove to be 'up', prior activity can be dropped and full orientation mobilized, followed by coping behaviour. (9) Note, the central thesis here is Darwininian. (10) If individuals were not highly responsive to hints of danger or opportunity, they would not be responsive enough; if they carried this response far on every occasion of its occurrence, they would spend all their time in a dither and have no time for all the other things required for survival.

Here the particular - if unremarkable - feature that I want to draw attention to is the rhetorical power of *lists*. Again, it is characteristic of a paratactic mode of writing that example should be piled upon example, and lists strung out. Goffman's lists here are striking. The first, in (2), refers to a collection of mundane functions and activities. It is, however, constructed in such a way as to generate its own extraordinary significance. The choice of words and their arrangement invests them with an almost liturgical weight. The list is marked by assonance and rhyme: *grazing, gazing, digesting, resting, playing, placidly....* which is continued alliteratively (*managed matters*).

The organization of this paragraph itself mirrors in style its subject-matter. The proposition that there are two fundamental modes of activity is (a) reflected in the construction of two contrasting lists, and (b) the syntax of the juxtaposed lists mirrors the two opposed 'modes'. The first list of activities is expressed in terms of a series of participles, each of which echoes the others, as well as the mores specific assonances and rhymes already referred to. The second, in (3), is very different: '... fully mobilized, a fury of intent, alarmed, they get ready to attack or to stalk or to flee'. The listing is more varied, the cadence more fractured, the verb forms more active. Routine, continuing activity is thus juxtaposed with the sudden punctuation of the non-routine and emergency. The listing style is of course continued in the next paragraph - *smells, sounds, sights, touches, pressures* - where the concatenation of specific terms is preferred to a more generic formulation - say 'the five senses'. It is entirely characteristic of Goffman's prose that lists of this sort should proliferate, and should be more common than formal definitions and propositions.

In this particular essay Goffman will in fact go on to formulate a more 'definitional' approach, in paragraph three:

> (11) When the world immediately around the individual portends nothing out of the ordinary, when the world appears to allow him to continue his routines (being indifferent to his designs and neither a major help nor a major hindrance), we can say that he will sense that appearances are 'natural' or 'normal'. (12) For the individual, then, normal appearances mean that it is safe and sound to continue on with the activity at hand with only peripheral attention given to checking up on the stability of the environment.

In introducing this 'definition' Goffman does so in a way characteristic of his paratactic mode. The 'definition' of 'normal appearances' is produced in a somewhat 'low-key' way. The terms have already been introduced and exemplified. The sentence in which the thematic phrase 'normal appearances' makes its first appearance (in that form) other than in the title of the essay simply recapitulates the earlier terms, so that the phrase itself seems to emerge 'naturally' out of the flow of descriptions and exemplars.

Of course, Goffman produces definitions, and of course there are propositions to be found in the work. Lofland's essay on Goffman's style makes just this point (Lofland 1980). He remarks that

> there are very many empirical assertions of the order 'X exists', but these are not propositions in the narrow theoretical sense. Rather, I am asking, are there propositions in the sense of assertions containing two concepts (or variables) said to be correlated? There do not seem to be many, but they do occur. They are difficult to find, at first, because they are not stated as explicit hypotheses. *They emerge as the overall argument of a paper or section that has been devoted to documenting kinds of things.* (Lofland, 1980, p. 33, my emphasis)

The sorts of propositions that Lofland derives are of the following type, and the summarise key features of Goffman's sociology::

> *If* persons are embedded in situated activity systems, *then* they will inject other identities into the system to show that theyare not only what the situation implies.

> *If* persons are to abide by the rules of interaction and treat one another relaively well, *then* they must treat each other as ritually sacred objects.

> *If* a fostered impression is to survive, *then* the audience must exercise tact in receiving it.

105

These propositions, and others of the same ilk that Lofland identifies, are certainly recognisable as Goffman's, but it is remarakable just how bland and anaemic such derivations appear in contrast with the detailed ostensive definitions and exemplifications that embody Goffman's sociology. Moreover, as Lofland notes, they are largely *implicit* within such stretches of text. Moreover, they are largely empty when drained of their exemplars. Consider a couple of Lofland's further derivations:

> *If* persons are placed in total institutions, *then* their selves will be mortified.

> *If* persons are placed in total institutions, *then* they will develop secondary adjustments to protect themselves from the identity implications of the organisations's theory of human nature.

Without the famous listings of types of 'total institution' and the detailed exemplification of, say, the 'mortification of the self', then the definitions seem jejune to say the least. The propositions, the theories, are inscribed in the textual details and organization. It is one of great strengths of Goffman's texts, and one of their characteristic limitations, that the work is not readily decontextualized from its original textual manifestations. This, it seems to me, is the feature of the texts which provides for their so-called 'literary' quality more generally than just the oft-noted use of 'metaphor', important though that is.

Style and semiosis

The question remains: what, if any, special significance are we to atttach to Goffman's distinctive style? It has been suggested elsewhere in these essays, and in many sources beyond this volume, that the rhetorical features of any scholarly texts are to some degree constitutive of the 'theories' and 'analyses' they embody. The rhetoric of scholarship is no mere accidental ornament or trapping. Just as there is no non-rhetorical linguistic-cum-textual medium of expression, so texts' meanings are inscribed in their textual arrangements and devices.

So it is clearly not enough to conclude simply that Goffman's 'style' resides solely in his readability or even in his deft use of striking examples. I have not presented an exhaustive analysis and do not propose a definitive verdict. Throughout, by means of a few selected passages for commentary, I have emphasised the *paratactic* nature of Goffman's writing. I have argued that this may be even more fundamental than his use of metaphor, perspective by incongruity and the like. That particular view is derived from Roustang's analysis of Freud's style, and I want to urge the heuristic value of that for an understanding of Goffman.

Roustang accounts for the parataxis of *The Interpretation of Dreams* on two related grounds. First, Freud lacks a general theory which will permit the formulation of propositional arguments:

> We must emphasize that Freud cannot make proofs, that he cannot deduce, because he cannot trace the processes of the dream to the already known of a general psychology that does not exist. He can only establish correspondences between dream-processes and other psychical functions. Through a series of paratactic procedures he can weave the threads of his discoveries and make them appear as a fabric. (pp.18-19)

Secondly, as we have seen already, Roustang suggests that the dominant paratactic approach mirrors the 'regression' of the dream-state to infantilism, the archaic and the neuroses.

Now my point is *not* that the stylistic parallels imply identical empistemologies in the two authors. Rather that there are important and illuminating homologies. In the case of neither Freud nor Goffman should the absence of an explicit 'theoretical' apparatus be seen as a lack or omission. As we have seen, 'theory' is conveyed implicitly through the persuasive accumulation of paratactic devices. In both authors, the style is a direct embodiment of their subject-matter. In each text is inscribed the ever-proliferating play of *semiosis*.

As Bourdieu (1983) remarked of Goffman, 'Through the subtlest, most fugitive indices of social interaction, he grasped the logic of the *work of representation...*' (p.113). While it would be crass to reduce Goffman to any single perspective, there is little difficulty in arguing that throughout his multi-faceted writing, there is a recurrent obsession with the semiotics of everyday life. Whether it be the management of signified (identity) through the manipulation of signifiers (appearance/front), the dislocation of signifier and signified (stigma), Goffman's motif remains the work of *signification*. His is not a humanistic social psychology of persons. Quite the contrary: the person is dissolved into the diverse practices of speech and comportment. There is no stable core, only the ever-changing, self-reproducing process of semiosis. Everyday life is represented as a massive, collective accomplishment of *bricolage*. The text themselves are artifacts of bricolage. Ideal types are assembled by the accretion of what Edmondson (1984, chap. 2 *passim*) refers to as 'actual types'. These are themslves derived from a bewildering variety of sources. They are powerful textual elements in persuading the reader to Goffman's point of view. The juxtaposition and mingling of the exotic and the commonplace, the respectable and the deviant, the repugnant and the laudable, the popular and the scholarly simultaneously invites and challenges the reader's sympathetic involvement with the text.

The organization of the texts develops Goffman's perspectives through their very organization and style. As Williams notes, specifically in the context of his metaphorical usage:

The bulk of his concepts were generated, developed and elaborated through the use of metaphor.... Metaphor was used by Goffman not as imagery, nor for the purpose of merely embellishing some pre-existing text, but it was used *directly*, as a technique of research, and it is a commonplace to assert that he was a master of this trope. This was no accident of style of course, for metaphor is the most powerful of means to express the complexity of relations between concepts; not through adding power to language incrementally, but because it is itself constitutive of the power of language.... It is not then that Goffman's studies were made to appear innovative through the use of metaphor, but that his conceptual advances were accomplished in the only way possible, though the process of linguistic invention and development pressed into the service of a sociological perspective. (Williams, 1983, p.101)

As I have tried to indicate (by no means exhaustively) Goffman's stylistic accomplishments go beyond just the trope of metaphor. In a remarkably consistent fashion, Goffman's texts *represent* his sociology through their modes of writing. The social world as represented by Goffman is the social world as inscribed in the texts. As Manning notes in his own essay in this vein, this homology of social life and sociological text is acknowledged explicitly by Goffman, in *Frame Analysis* (1974) for example, where the self-referential and reflexive character of Goffman's writing is itself foregrounded as a topic for the author's 'Introduction' (esp. p.11 ff.). He acknowledges the following feature as characteristic of his own paratactic style:

The problem ... is that once a term is introduced (this occurring at the point at which it is first needed), it begins to have too much bearing, not merely applying to what comes later, but reapplying in each chapter to what it has already applied to. Thus each succeeding section of the study becomes more entangled, until a step can hardly be made because of what must be carried along with it. The process closely follows the horrors of repetition songs, as if - in the case of frame analysis - what Old MacDonald had on his farm were partridge and juniper trees.(Goffman, 1974, p. 11)

Old MacDonald is an excellent metaphor for Goffman's work in general. The repetition song parallels precisely the proliferation of exemplars and concepts, through the play of semiosis and the stylistic elaboration of his key metaphors and models.

8 The ethnography of a medical setting: reading, writing and rhetoric

Introduction: fieldnotes revisited

In this essay I aim simultaneously to reflect on methodological and substantive issues in the study of medical work and culture. Its central concern is with texts: the texts which we as social scientists ourselves generate in the course of our work, and the texts which are the work of members of a given culture under scrutiny. Briefly, the essay will look forward to an 'ethnopoetics' of medical cultures, while reflecting back on the poetics of our own ethnography.

As with many reflections on ethnographic fieldwork, the paper is autobiographical. It is not, however, intended to be a contribution to the highly personalized genre of 'confessional' accounts. Van Maanen (1988) has sketched some features of that genre, which includes some contributions relevant to health research, such as collections edited by Horobin and Davis (1977) and McKeganey and Cunningham-Burley (1987). I have already published several autobiographical descriptions of my ethnographic research, including an earlier chapter in this volume, and this chapter does not recapitulate their contents. The intention here is to take the opportunity to reflect on some specific issues of method.

At the beginning of my career I undertook ethnographic research in the Edinburgh medical school. On the basis of that work I completed a doctoral dissertation, published a monograph and a series of papers (cf. Atkinson, 1975, 1977b, 1981, 1988). At the end of any such project or series of projects (if indeed they can ever be said to end) one is always aware that the written products only represent possible versions. There is a dazzlingly large variety of ways in which the material could be organized, numerous perspectives that could be adopted, and a multiplicity of stories that could be told. Yet while we often continue to mine our data, we rarely go back to try out radically alternative versions, to see where they might lead. It is such an exercise - though modest in its scope - that I shall report on here.

109

In conducting the Edinburgh research I spread my fieldwork over two years. The practical and organization reasons for the actual conduct of the work need not detain us here, but the result was that I spent the first of those years observing the teaching of general medicine to students in their first year of clinical studies, and spent the second year observing the teaching of surgery to the next cohort of students, also in their first clinical year. Readers not familiar with medical education in Britain need to know that it occupies a minimum of five years of undergraduate study. In many medical schools, including Edinburgh at the time of my research, the curriculum divides between preclinical and clinical work. The students I worked with were in their third or fourth year of medical education. They had completed their preclinical studies in subjects such as Anatomy and Physiology. In the first clinical year they received bedside instruction in several teaching hospitals, in general medicine and general surgery, together with lectures and practical classes in clinical sciences.

It turned out that I wrote most of my thesis and publications on that first year of fieldwork - in general medicine. The reasons for that are not laudable, but are, in retrospect, understandable. To begin with, I found it all too easy to be unduly swayed by the medical students' own frequently stated preference for medicine over surgery. The students and I tended to find the general 'atmosphere' (as they called it) of surgical wards much less engaging and welcoming than that of the medical side. Moreover, the clinical work in medicine often proved (again, to the students and me) to be more intellectually engaging and taxing than that in surgery. Paradoxically, in contrast to lay stereotypes and students' expectations, there was less 'action' in surgery. The students themselves felt they were too passive in surgery, and had too little opportunity for work with patients. These student evaluations of learning experiences and 'atmospheres' in different specialties have been documented elsewhere (e.g. Atkinson 1977c).

Despite my best endeavours to avoid the adoption of members' perspectives, I tended to feel more engaged and absorbed with the work of general medicine. This was enhanced by the fact that I had studied medicine first. Although I like to think that I strove constantly to reflect upon the data I was collecting, and the lines of inquiry I was exploring, in retrospect it is evident that most of the lines of inquiry were established during the first year of the research. The second year was by no means a total write-off. Yet there is no doubt that in terms of my overall work, the second year in surgery was not used to the best possible advantage. At worst, a good deal of the work seemed redundant - adding relatively little to existing themes and categories, other than their extension to new social contexts.

The upshot is that my fieldnotes in surgery remain all but unpublished. Regretting that state of affairs, I decided to return to those old field note books. Though they are now very old, it seemed that they still might contain something of interest. Quite apart from any other considerations, it remains the case that very few people have written sociologically about medical education in Britain, and there is also relatively little written about surgery. A recent exception in Britain is Fox (1991), who has published a substantial and innovatory ethnography of surgical practice. There have of course been notable sociological studies of surgery in the United States, most notably Bosk (1979), Burkett and Knafl (1974), Knafl and Burkett (1975) and Katz (1984, 1985). These publications all appeared after the completion of my own surgery fieldwork. Given the relative paucity of sociological research in the area, it seemed that my own data should not be wasted altogether.

We know relatively little about the construction and interpretation of fieldnotes in ethnographic research. In recent years cultural anthropologists have begun to explore the issue, however. Sanjek (1990) has collected a series of autobiographical, reflective accounts by anthropologists on the use of their own and others' fieldnotes. They all, in various ways, highlight the fact that the 'fieldnote' is not a closed, determinate text. The social scientist must recognize that the fieldnote is what Jackson (1990) calls a 'liminal text', constantly available for interpretation and reinterpretation.

It is clear that my own fieldnotes are in no sense complete records of what I observed 'in the field'. They are very partial records. They 'made sense' when they were written, and make sense now, insofar as I bring to bear my tacit knowledge of those settings, and can evoke general and particular features of them. They also make sense in that I bring to them sociological interests whereby meaning and significance may be read into them.

What now strikes me as I review the notebooks is that I find contrasting possible ways of doing that reading. And we have to bear in mind at this juncture in the argument that in doing the kind of work I am referring to, we are engaged in complex processes of writing and reading. The construction of fieldnotes, diaries and the like, reading and re-reading those documents, writing analytic notes and memos, working papers, theses, journal articles and monographs - these all imply completed processes of textual construction and interpretation.

These remarks all bear, therefore, on more general concerns about the reading and writing of ethnographic texts. In recent years sociologiusts and anthropologists have become increasingly aware of the 'literary' character of their accounts. It is now widely acknowledged that ethnographers need to reflect not only on their methods of data collection and analysis, but on their methods of reading and writing too (cf. Atkinson, 1990, 1991, 1992; Hammersley 1991; Van Maanen, 1988). Here no attempt is made to address all the issues raised in that now extensive literature (e.g. Agar, 1990; Boon, 1982; Clifford and Marcus, 1986; Clifford 1988; Edmondson 1984; Fabian 1983; Geertz 1988; Richardson 1990; Wolcott 1990). Rather, I shall try to reflect on two different strategies of reading ethnographic fieldnotes. I shall not be proposing the superiority of one or other of the two approaches.

The first reading strategy approximates to the sort of methodological orthodoxy one finds enshrined in standard textbooks on ethnographic methods. As Tesch (1990) suggests, it is based on 'de-contextualizing' and 're-contextualizing' data (cf. Bogdan and Biklen 1982; Hammersley and Atkinson 1983; Lofland 1971). It owes a good deal to the 'culture of analysis' shared by many methodological approaches. It derives from that well-established style of work whereby the data are inspected for categories and instances. It is an approach which disaggregates the text (notes or transcripts) into a series of fragments, which are then re-grouped under a series of thematic headings. In a practical sense this is often a matter of physical fragmentation. The actual technology employed may vary: from computer storage and retrieval to punch cards and knitting needles, to file cards, to cardboard shoe boxes, to manilla folders.

Lofland (1971) provides a classic example of such procedural advice. He recommends that in addition to preserving a complete, chronologically ordered account, one should get 'the material out of the sheer chronological narrative of one's field or interview notes and into a flexible storage, ordering and retrieval format'. Lofland goes on to recommend the establishment and use of different sorts of files. Files can be maintained relating to people, places, organizations, events and so on. Sets of analytic files physically embody the data relating to emergent, developing themes. The internal ordering of such analytic files, of their progressive fragmentation into increasing numbers of sub-files, is a representation of the developing delicacy and complexity of the analytic framework. The analytic task, therefore, resolves itself - at a practical level - into the construction of classes or categories, and the sorting of data into them.It was a fairly crude, manual, version of this approach that I adopted in my own Edinburgh research. In retrospect it was perhaps 'floppy' rather than 'flexible' and 'vague' rather than 'tentative'. It did, however, prove adequately robust for the purposes of organizing the material and my thinking.

The majority of younger scholars will now be more familiar with microcomputer software that is used to perform essentially the same tasks. The varieties of text analysis programs that are in common use all rest on the basic procedure of 'tagging' or 'coding' segments of data (fieldnotes, transcripts etc.), searching for coded segments, and gathering together equivalent segments (Tesch 1990). The use of microcomputing software thus allows the ethnographer to search his or her data more quickly, more systematically and more comprehensively. For the most part, however, the strategies employed are conceptually the same as manual techniques for fragmentation and filing. It is virtually the same exercise - cutting up the text and re-ordering it into analytic files (cf Weaver and Atkinson 1994).

By way of exemplification, here is just one collection of terms under which data extracts were identified and collected. The most general heading for this collection of data was 'medical knowledge'. (This superordinate category was, of course, too broad to imply any analytic cutting edge of its own.) Under this heading were filed all extracts from clinical teaching episodes and interviews which related to definitions and perceptions of the state of medical knowledge, its limitations and its complexities, its warrants and legitimacy. Specific key words included: Uncertainty; Judgment; Complexity. Their contents were derived from previously published accounts in the sociology of medicine and of professional socialization, as well as from my readings of my own data. I wove the data from this collection of categories into various published accounts of the reproduction of medical knowledge, and on the discourse of 'uncertainty', 'dogmatism', 'judgement' and 'personal experience' (cf. Atkinson, 1984b).

The following extracts from my surgery fieldnotes will give some idea of the sort of material gathered in this file. I made the following notes during a discussion about a patient with a thyroid problem. The consultant surgeon Mr Mackay, summarized the case to the group of junior students:

Cons: So there's an example, of course, of a goitre in a patient of thirty-six, of long standing. So you are in a little difficulty if it isn't nodular. You've finished with thyroid pathology?
Stud: Yes
Cons: So what is it?
Stud: If it isn't nodular, it might be adenoma of the thyroid.
Cons: Hmmm; I sometimes think that pathologists have a distorted view of thyroid pathology. By adenoma I suppose you mean a simple tumour.
Stud: Yes
Cons: Simple tumours of the thyroid are *very* rare.
Mr.Mackay then went on to ask the students about the age of onset of goitre:
Stud: Onset of puberty
Cons: You're quite right that the text-books talk of adolescent goitre, but....
And he then went on to tell the students that in practice things are rather different from what the text-books say.

This particular extract is reproduced in my book (Atkinson 1981). It is in fact one of the few extracts from the surgery data to appear in print. There I use it to illustrate two closely related features. The first is the way in which clinicians make passing reference to the non-clinical instruction the students may or may not have received: 'You've finished with thyroid pathology?' (This sort of inquiry is often made with an almost studied air of indifference). The second is the way in which clinicians contrast clinical knowledge and experience with text-book knowledge or the views of non-clinical specialists.

Published with that extract is one taken from my notes made when that same patient was being operated on, the following day. The students and I were gathered, gowned and masked, in an open observation gallery above the operating table. As the consultant was in the middle of the operation he said to us:

> This is the point of the operation at which there's a little mess, unfortunately, because we have an unsutured stump of thyroid.... The classic, text-book way of removing the thyroid is ... (and he described it briefly) ... Garside here in Edinburgh was responsible for modifying it in the way we've been doing it this morning. It doesn't give you such a pretty specimen, but it gives you a better idea of what you've taken away and what's left.

Here again, this was indexed to categories of 'text-book' pronouncements, with additional cross-reference to invocations of 'local' preferences, traditions and so on. The latter would include cross-reference to instances such as the following:

> The surgeon was discussing a patient with breast cancer: 'In this city she'd have a simple mastectomy'. He explained to the students the difference between simple and radical mastectomies. 'In Edinburgh, it's accepted that most units do a simple mastectomy.'

Examples of this sort, then, were collected together, with numerous others, of course, to generate a series of major analytic themes in the work. Those unremarkable analytic procedures were carried out quite adequately. The surgery fieldnotes, when reviewed, do not suggest any radical change in the implementation of that particular approach. In essence it seems a sensible and robust approach. It generated productive enough ideas at the time and subsequently. Indeed, on re-reading the surgery notes I initially found it difficult to *escape* those categories I had initially established: understandably, they furnished a powerful conceptual grid. Moreover, they exercised a more physical constraint. The notes as I confronted them had been fragmented into the constituent themes.

If I were to attempt an extended write-up of the data now, of course, I should draw on different - or at least additional - sources and ideas. I realise, for instance, that my account of 'textbook' versus 'practical' knowledge would have been greatly enhanced with reference to Ludwik Fleck (1979), for instance. His extraordinarily prescient book only became widely available in translation after the completion of my research. It contains a perceptive discussion of the contrasts between 'journal science', 'textbook science', 'vademecum science' and 'popular science'. Its relevance for an understanding of medical knowedge and medical science is profound. The sociology of medicine and the sociology of science have progressed in the years since my original fieldwork, and a thorough analysis would now need to take full account of the respective bodies of literature. Nevertheless, there was nothing inherently wrong with what I began to do with those surgery fieldnotes, or what I would have continued to do with them had I found time and opportunity to proceed.

What became interesting for me, therefore, was the re-ordering of those notes, or, to be more precise, the suspension of such an analytic mode. Rather than working on the filed and indexed fragments, I have gone back to the original notebooks. This has proved an interesting exercise in re-reading; and it is to that I shall now turn.

In the first place, the notes themselves are very patchy. There must have been a host of more or less implicit decisions which influenced what I noted, and how I did it. Some of the notes are left as 'jottings' - brief notes consisting only of key words, phrases and fragments of conversation. They were scribbled down 'in the field' or immediately afterwards. Others are worked up into 'processed' notes, with more extended reconstructions of scenes, actions and words (cf. Hammersley and Atkinson 1983, pp. 145-161). The extended, polished notes were written up away from 'the field', usually later the same day.

The notes are evocative (cf Lederman 1990). Incomplete though they are, they trigger a variety of memories: with no guarantee, of course, that those 'memories' are faithful reconstructions of what actually occurred. The written record and memory interact to produce new reconstructions of social settings and persons. Some characters can still be 'heard' and conjured up; others remain shadowy. Unnamed individuals make fleeting contributions and are now quite lost to view. In some ways, after the passage of time the notes are alien in some ways. One comes to them 'cold'. Reading them is, however, different from the reported experience of working with someone else's field data (Lutkehaus 1990). For they can still evoke a lived experience.

The fragmentation of the original notes reflects the previous work I had done. It prefigures the 'cutting up' of the fieldnotes for analytic purposes. The categories I had developed during my year of general medicine exerted their influence. For much of the time the notes themselves seem to display a tunnel vision, implicitly recapitulating the pre-existing frameworks. What I find on re-reading is that I am now much less inclined to fragment the notes into relatively small segments. Instead, I am just as interested in reading episodes and passages at greater length, with a correspondingly different attitude towards the act of reading, and hence of analysis. Rather than constructing my account like a patchwork quilt, I feel more like working with the whole cloth.

To be more precise, what now concerns me is the nature of these products as *texts*, and the nature of the 'texts' they report (and distort) and comment on. In particular, what now strikes me is the extent to which the scenes and actions which are represented, or hinted at, there - display a variety of spoken performances - largely, but not exclusively, by the clinical teachers. What now engages my attention, then, is the *rhetoric* of medical accounts and presentations, rather than fragmenting episodes into small shreds and patches. In the following section I shall attempt to illustrate that approach more concretely.

The surgeon's story

The following extract from my surgery fieldnotes, serves to illustrate the general point.

> Mr Jenkins summarized the patient's case from the folder of notes. His aim, he said, was to show that even what he called 'straightforward surgery' is 'not always so straightforward'. It had been thought that the patient - a man of 69 - had some inflammation of the gall-bladder. He had been brought in to have an oral cholecystogram. The report had been made that 'There is no evidence of a functioning gall bladder'.
>
> 'This as far as we are concerned confirmed our diagnosis of cholecystitis'.
>
> He was therefore admitted to have his gall bladder removed: 'a very routine decision'. At operation an investigation had been carried out - an operative cholecystogram. There was no stone found in the bile duct, but there was no flux into the gall bladder. A T-tube (drain) was inserted and the patient sent back to the ward. On the third postoperative day it was noticed that the patient was jaundiced. This could have arisen from an obstruction of the bile duct, or from a diseased liver. On the eighth postoperative day there was further investigation of the bile duct; this suggested that there *was* a stone in the duct.
>
> The patient had appeared to be getting better, but he had a sudden episode of collapse. He was operated on and found to have a large collection of blood and bile, which had led to septicaemia.
>
> On the twelfth postoperative day the patient started to leak clear fluid through the main wound. His wounds had broken down, and he was taken to theatre and stitched again.
>
> On the fourteenth day the patient had a fever and a high white blood cell count. He developed pneumonia, which cleared up with antibiotics.
>
> Then suddenly, the patient had vomited old, dark blood. Soon after he had also vomited bright fresh blood. He lost several pints of blood. He was operated on by a senior surgeon, who could find no reason for the bleeding. A vagotomy and pyloroplasty were performed.
>
> Two nights ago the patient had collapsed again. 'We think he's got another septicaemia... He's very far from well and there's no guarantee that he'll pull through....
>
> This man represents the very end of the scale. Mortality from cholecystectomy is 0.5 per cent. In any centre like this it ought

116

to be virtually nil. It's not easy to point the blame.'

Under my original schema, this extract, or fragments of it, could have been used to document and illustrate several of the related themes referred to above. It could have been indexed to link of 'unpredictability' with 'uncertainty', 'patient career', 'trajectory' and so on. There would also have been cross-reference to the local reputation and standing of Edinburgh as a centre of excellence. There are, however, other things to be said about the material. In note form, with a mixture of summary, indirect and direct speech, the data are clearly far from ideal. Nevertheless, they do enough to indicate a different line of approach, which is more concerned with the *narrative form* it reflects. The case is presented by the surgeon as a story, and is a particular sort of story at that. The surgeon reveals the growing catalogue and complexities of the unfortunate patient's troubles through a narrative unfolding, ordered on a chronological basis. Reference to this as a 'narrative' event draws attention to the complex relationship between 'events', their organization into a 'story', and the 'performance' of that narrative to an audience. Bauman (1986) outlines the relationship between those three elements in oral discourse, and emphasizes the extent to which the 'story' shapes 'events' rather than events determining stories. A spoken narrative is one of several ways in which a medical 'case' may be assembled, shaped and shared. (cf. Kleinman 1988). The complication in this instance is that the 'surgeon's story' is embedded and represented in the written text of my own narratives - the fieldnotes.

As a story we could loosely relate it to a collection of formats or genres of spoken and written narratives. This particular story has affinities with styles of story and legend whereby simple and straightforward beginnings proceed by an apparently inexorable series of steps to culminate in a concatenation of complications and misfortunes. The force of such catalogues of tribulation can be comic or horrific. Many modern urban legends combine the two into a sort of ghoulish black humour. ('Urban legends' are a class of stories that circulate widely, are often half-believed, and are often attributed to a 'friend of a friend': see Brunvand, 1983, 1984, 1985; Delamont 1989, 1991).

The particular story under consideration here has another quality: it could be likened to a 'mystery' or 'cliff-hanger'. Although a resolution is projected in the clinician's gloomy prognostication, the story is contrived in such a way as to build up to a crisis or suspense-like climax. It is, furthermore, a story with a moral or several morals. The surgeon foreshadowed that in his own preface to the story, telling the students that he was going to use the case to illustrate that 'straightforward' surgery is not always so. It is a morality story which deals with blame, or its absence, and the fateful hazards of surgical work. (cf.Bosk 1979).

In other words, without too much imagination we can see that here we are dealing with an artfully ordered account which relies on some basic - but nonetheless important - narrative skills on the part of the surgeon. It is important to remember that although the clinician had the folder of case notes open on his knee, he was not simply reading off the story from such written documents. His story was an extempore production, which wove the disparate bits and pieces of the case notes into a coherent account. There were many different 'stories' or 'versions' he could have constructed on the basis of those raw materials.

In this instance the surgeon has created a particular kind of narrative which has elements of the genre known as the 'atrocity story' (cf. Dingwall 1977). This is a particular kind of morality tale, widely documented in medical and other settings. The atrocity story is a widespread type of occupational narrative in which is enshrined tales of gross incompetence, appalling consequences and dire penalties. Atrocity stories have much in common with urban legends, and particular 'atrocities' may take on legendary status in the oral culture of an occupational group. Such stories often draw, as here, upon formats of 'contrastive rhetoric' (cf. Hargreaves 1981). That is, the description or narrative of a case or of a state of affairs is constructed on the basis of contrasts (explicit or implicit) between 'what we do here' and 'what goes on elsewhere'. As in this instance, the atrocity story is a powerful means for the transmission and inculcation of occupational values and rhetoric.

If we reconstruct the surgeon's story from the fieldnote account, then we can also analyse it from a more structural perspective. We can look for the elementary components of this particular 'story'. In summary form they are:

> The Preface and foreshadowed Moral; the initial Problem (diagnosis); Action (operation); Complications (jaundice, no gall stones); Mystery (gall stone after all); further Complication and Crisis (sudden collapse, septicaemia, wound break down, fever, vomiting blood; renewed Action (further operations); more Complications; Resolution (foreshadowed but hanging in the balance; Moral re-stated.

We know from other studies of narratives that they have some common features and formats. The sequence captured in the notes can be examined from this point of view. The perspective provided by Labov and his collaborators (Labov 1972; Labov and Waletzky 1967) suggests that the 'surgeon's story' has similarities with a wider class of narrative performances. Labov derives from his analysis of spoken narratives the following elements:

(1) Abstraction: story summary
(2) Orientation: e.g. time and place
(3) Complication action
(4) Evaluation
(5) Result or resolution
(6) Coda

118

These elemental structures and functions can be worked into patterns of differing complexity, embeddedness and sequential ordering. The important thing is the fact that narrative structures themselves are used to give shape, coherence, consequence, newsworthiness, drama, suspense and morality to the events they report.

The surgeon's narrative just referred to is a member of a general class of 'case' accounts. The case presentation is a very pervasive type of narrative performance in medical (and other) settings (cf. Pithouse, 1985). Case talk is done in a variety of contexts, with different purposes, and with different audiences. Those range from the most fleeting and informal sharing of information, through daily working rounds, teaching rounds, weekly mortality and morbidity reviews, 'conferences', and 'grand rounds'. A case which, by reason of complexity, newsworthiness or rarity, excites the curiosity of physicians may be 'presented' in all such contexts over the span of the patient's hospital admission.

Medical work and medical instruction interweave spoken accounts and practical tasks in the daily routines of 'rounds' and consultations. A further extended example from the surgery fieldnotes illustrates the point, while further exemplifying the 'extended' reading strategy. The following extract is taken from an even longer record. It begins in the course of a small group teaching session, taking place in a teaching room attached to one of the surgery firms. A consultant surgeon, Mr Walker, is talking to a small group of students:

> Mr Walker looked at his watch, and said that he had to go down at about half past, in a moment or two. He then took us down to one of the small female wards. It was occupied by one patient. Mr Walker explained that he had to take a blood sample from her: he did so. He showed us that she had a canula in her left arm, and told us that she had to have frequent samples removed: having the canula in is much less painful than having the arm pricked all the time.
>
> One of the students, quite spontaneously, asked the patient if it was at all uncomfortable. She replied that it was 'a bit sore', at which Mr Walker seemed rather concerned, and examined the arm where the canula was inserted.
>
> Angela Oakley [one of the students] asked if the patient could bend her arm with the canula in position. Mr Walker said that the canula can stand a few bends, but the patient should not bend her arm if she could help it. Mr Walker also told the students that tomorrow she had to have tests every quarter of an hour, sixteen times in all: 'I'm sure she'd rather have the canula in for that than have her arm pricked all the time.'
>
> Mr Walker then led us out of the side ward and, very briefly, gave us a guided tour. He indicated the female ward at the end of

the short corridor, and pointed out the teaching, adding that, of course, we knew that already. As he led the way out and across· the corridor he opened a cupboard door and showed us where the microscope was kept - just in case anybody should ever tell one of the students to go and do something they needed the microscope for.

As he took us through to the men's ward, Mr Walker indicated a side room. We all peered in as we passed. All we could see were some screens, and a few people sitting outside in the corridor. Mr Walker explained that it was here that the Unit performed its gastric function tests. He went on to explain that they themselves used a test that had been developed here by the Unit, rather than the usual test. He wasn't sure, he added, if any of the other units in the hospital were using this yet.

He also indicated the ward sister's room as we passed into the entrance to the main men's ward. By the bed immediately to our left, a man was sitting in his armchair. He had a nasogastric tube, and a number of other tubes and plastic bags draped about him. His belly was heavily plastered, and he looked very disconsolate indeed.

We spent the rest of the time talking generally about this patient, and about some general problems. Mr Walker talked about the use of the nasogastric tube. He explained that after the stomach or gut has been handled or disturbed, then it cannot empty properly and has to be emptied via the tube. Previously, the contents of the stomach had been vomited up after operations. This had been dangerous, as it could lead to the vomit being inhaled and leading to an inhalation pneumonia.

Mr Walker took the patient's chart and pointed out a postoperative temperature rise. He described this as a normal postoperative reaction. He pointed out that in the space above the temperature on the chart was an 'E'. He asked the students what they thought that might refer to. Somebody volunteered a wrong answer. Mr Walker reminded them that the space was for recording antibiotics, and another of the students correctly volunteered 'Erythromycin'.

Mr Walker explained that he was generally against the use of antibiotics if at all possible, and would prefer to combat chest infection with physiotherapy, but others would more readily prescribe. He commented that this demonstrated how medicine was largely 'opinion based' and therefore could not lay claim to being 'an exact science'.

When Mr Walker had finished teaching the students, he had to return to the first patient to take another blood sample. The students, not having been formally dismissed, followed him along and stood watching him. He was obviously rather surprised and taken aback to find that the students were still following him....

Once again, it is easy to see how fragments from this more extended extract could be 'coded' into a series of thematic elements. Sections clearly relate to themes of 'opinion', 'local practice' and the like. They are clearly relevant to a general interest in the sociology of medical knowledge. From that perspective, the 'fragmentation' strategy would clearly be adequate, and the data perfectly usable. Equally, however, one can learn something from a more extended reading of the full fieldnote. In contrast to the 'narrative' performance captured in the previous extract, the episode reported here is itself more disjointed. It does not report a single 'case' or a single 'story'. What it does illustrate is how instructional talk and medical work are interwoven, and how educational relevance is *improvised* from the tasks and materials at hand to the clinician. The surgeon's actions are governed by the requirements of his clinical responsibilities, such as the frequent sampling for the testing of blood gases from the first patient. Having had to take the students from the teaching room, the surgeon then improvises a mini-tour of the ward environment (the students were in their first few days on that surgical attachment), and he generates an impromptu instructional session until it is necessary for him to return to the first patient.

Here, then, the rhetorical skills that are illustrated are intricately linked to physical movement through the clinical space of the wards. They are, moreover, tied to the observation of physical objects attached to, inserted into, or in proximity to, the patient's body. This is a highly characteristic aspect of surgical teaching. The fieldnote rather nicely captures some of the technology (in the broadest sense) of surveillance of modern surgical practice. Finally, the extended reading of the extract gives the reader a clear sense - which escapes finer fragmentation - of the 'procession' that takes surgeon and students through clinical space. The students are taken on a 'guided tour' of the surgical unit. The physical distribution of patients and medical tasks in that apace provides occasion for the play of the 'clinical gaze' (cf Foucault 1976; Atkinson 1981; Armstrong 1983). As the teaching round proceeds, the students can inspect - even just in passing - patients and the physical manifestation of their respective conditions or treatments. We saw in the discussion of the 'surgeon's story' that the 'case' is the pretext for a 'morality tale', in which the surgeon draws out a general conclusion. In this second extract too we can see how the surgeon derives the general from the particular. Starting from an observation of the individual patient, he moves to a more general statement concerning his preference for the management of chest infection. He then moves to another level of generality with a statement about the very nature of medical knowledge itself. The structure of the narrative discourse thus encodes a more general pattern of medical thought, inference and work, grounded in 'the case'.

Medical work and medical talk

As has already been acknowledged, the fieldnote is an imperfect record. These extracts, though quite carefully written up, do not capture all of the potentially relevant speech and action. They omit, because they take for granted, much detail about the physical arrangements of the setting. A fully realized analysis would call for more detailed reconstructions and descriptions in order to produce a comprehensive and comprehensible account. Nevertheless, they do allow the analyst to recapture and to comment on a number of important actions.

The second of the extended extracts illustrates how the discourse of surgery may grow out of and accompany physical activities. It alerts us to a general type of medical talk: the 'commentary'. In the surgical context, of course, this form of talk is most vividly exemplified in the talk that accompanies the performance of an operation or a procedure in the clinical or the theatre. The commentary is addressed to students and colleagues in order to explain, justify, prompt and to give context to the taasks of surgical work.

On reflection, it is apparent that in something like a medical setting there are many contexts in which stories and accounts of this sort may be produced. Different social contexts, with different audiences and different medical tasks at hand may evoke narratives with differing properties. Indeed, one of the most striking things about some medical settings is the sheer amount of *talk* that is generated. Medical *work* involves not only the 'direct' diagnosis and management of individual patients, but also the transformation of such work into accounts of it. The construction of the 'case' is discursive work which is fundamental to the tasks of sharing, communicating, informing, debating and monitoring between members of the medical profession, and between physicians and others. The tendency of social scientists is to focus on doctor-patient interaction, with the consequence that such features of everyday work are often overlooked. Several major studies of medical discourse have documented interactional features of medical encounters in considerable detail (cf. Fisher and Todd, 1983; West 1984; Mishler 1984; Heath 1986; Silverman 1987). By contrast, doctor-doctor interaction has not received the same degree of attention. Yet the accomplishment of medical work, of many kinds, is achieved through rhetorical skills and routines of many kinds.

Kleinman (1988) has documented how illness may be constructed through narrative. He concentrates on the experience of the patient. But it is also the work of the medical practitioner, who also produces stories and other forms of talk to give shape and consequence to the 'disease' and its treatment. Mishler (1984) has attempted to identify two 'voices' that mutually interrupt one another in the course of the consultation - the 'voice of the lifeworld' and the 'voice of medicine'. The voice of the lifeworld is, in Mishler's view, primarily that which is articulated by the patient; it is couched in narrative format and is biographical in its point of view. The voice of medicine, though not exclusively the province of the physician, is oriented to the de-contextualized meanings of biomedical science. But Mishler's dichotomous analysis is too simple. So-called biomedicine is itself expressed in a variety of narrative formats. Physicians and surgeons tell and re-tell their cases to each other and to their students. The 'case' *is* the telling: the medical 'history' is aptly named. There is no doubt that the narratives of medical practitioners transform the narratives of their lay clients. The patient's illness is grounded in his or her biographical ordering of events. The doctor's narrative of the patient's illness is grounded in his or her own occupational biography - as evidence of 'experience' and 'judgment' - and the moral of the tale is to be found in a medical frame of reference. Nevertheless, it is vital for sociologists of medical work to recognize its production in spoken performance. There remains considerable work to be done if our 'thick descriptions' of medical settings are to do justice to the rhetoric of the clinic. Elsewhere (Atkinson 1995) I have tried to explore more systematically and more methodically how the rhetorical forms and rituals of clinical life are used to construct and convey clinical fats, findings and opinions in the day-to-day interactions between medical practitioners and their professional colleagues. The clinical skills of medical practice, and the scientific skills of laboratory medical science are mediated by the rhetorical skills of the clinic (Atkinson 1994).

Conclusion

In the course of this essay an attempt has been made to consider alternative methods of reading and interpreting the same set of ethnographic 'data'. Two strategies for treating fieldnotes have been outlined. The first approach is characteristic of the 'culture of fragmentation' that informs a great deal of contemporary qualitative analysis. It is a well established approach which has many benefits and applications. It is dependent on the 'cut-and-paste' disaggregation of the original field data. The data fragments are thus 'de-contextualized' and then 're-contextualized' into overarching analytic themes and categories. The strategy, however, does lose important aspects of the 'reality' of the field. The culture of fragmentation too readily lends itself to the de-contextualization of data and its aggregation in ways that implicitly recapitulate positivist assumptions (cf Dey 1995).

An alternative approach to reading is proposed. Rather than the fragmentation of the field data, this strategy attempts to pay more attention to the structure of the 'texts of the field'. It recognizes two things. First, the fieldnotes are themselves textual products. Secondly, they report and incorporate rhetorical accomplishments on the part of the social actors. Attention to those two features of the 'data' has implications for analysis. It encourages us to realise that the 'data' with which we deal are open, intermediate texts with which the analyst interacts, where meaning is made rather than found. Further, it leads us to a recognition of how social action -

here, medical work - is accomplished through narrative and other verbal performances.

The two strategies of reading are, of course, complementary. For the purposes of argument I have rather exaggerated the differences here. They are not contrasted in order to advocate one and denigrate the other. My purpose has rather been to draw attention to several things. In the first place, it is important to realise that, just as 'data' are not fixed, so there is no one best way of reading them. On the contrary, there is every advantage in canvassing different approaches. Secondly, there is merit in trying different analytic strategies on the same ethnographic data. We engage too rarely in secondary analyses or meta-analyses of ethnographic materials. There may be much to be learned from such methodological exercises. Third, the exercise forces us to treat our taken-for-granted methods and analyses as problematic. We should not fall into analytic approaches that are employed routinely, mechanistically and uncritically. Given the current popularity of certain computer-based analytic strategies, a constant questioning of our analytic practices is especially important and timely.

These seem to be the advantages of this kind of retrospective, autobiographical account. It is possible to engage in the critical reflection we expect of all qualitative researchers. We do so not in order to indulge in narcissism, nor in order to confess our past sins. The point is to learn about methodological principles that can inform future work for ourselves and others.

9 Reading health economics

Introduction

This essay is not intended to be a comprehensive introduction to the discipline of health economics. It is not even a systematic review of literature in that field. Rather, it contains a reflection on the exercise of reading a strange corpus of academic material. It is thus an exercise in reading - from the perspective of a sociologist - rather than a synoptic critique of the discipline. As I explained in the introduction to this volume, it is derived from a very particular exercise. As part of a joint conference, I was asked to read a selection of texts in health economics and to provide a commentary on them. In producing the reading contained in this essay, I clearly transgressed some of the expectations that lay behind that conference. It was part of the implicit agenda of that occasion that members of the two disciplines, who ostensibly common ground between us, and to seek out shared interests. There was clearly an expectation that a constructive dialogue should take place and that the outcome should be an agenda for joint activity. In the event I found it almost impossible to move directly to such a synthetic perspective. In undertaking the task I started (and clearly ended) as a complete novice in health economics. I therefore decided to make the best of that circumstance, and thus to make a virtue of necessity. I therefore suggest that my position as a complete outsider provided a particularly valuable stance from which to address the various prescribed fragments of academic discourse. My difficulties as a naive reader therefore provide the starting point for my exercise in reading.

That general stance, of course, is congruent with my broader interests in sociology and the sociology of textual practices. I thus place myself, for the purposes of these texts, as the ethnographic outsider, adopting the stance of what Lofland (1971) described as a 'socially acceptable incompetent'. Intellectually, whether based on ethnographic fieldwork or on the reading of texts, this involves a commitment to making the familiar seem strange and the strange seem familiar. In tackling this particular exercise, I did not of course engage in direct fieldwork with health economists, as others have done (Ashmore et al. 1989), but engaged with published texts. But the attitude adopted is essentially similar. As a sociologist, I treated the particular exercise in cross-disciplinary reading as the equivalent to the exploration of an alien culture. It is thus equivalent to an anthropological inquiry. There is a constant dialectical process of reflection as one engages with a chosen culture or sub-culture in the course of research. On the one hand, one confronts novelty and puzzlement: one strives to understand and account for the strange. On the other hand, one is simultaneously forced to confront, actually or in imagination, one's own cherished beliefs and assumptions.

The outsider

In this encounter with health economics, then, I find myself approaching the task as a complete outsider. I am in that position that the phenomenologist Alfred Schutz (1964) ascribed to the 'outsider' or the 'stranger'. Schutz's original essay was ostensibly an exercise in the social psychology of groups. His portrayal of the archetypal stranger stands as a metaphor for the phenomenologically-inspired philosopher or social scientist. Of the stranger Schutz (1964: 98) wrote: 'He becomes essentially the man [sic] who has to place in question nearly everything that seems to be unquestionable to the members of the approached group'. The stranger thus finds that his or her habitual modes of thought are alien to those of the newly encountered group. Thus, both cultures become problematic and available for scrutiny. Schutz (p.99) continued:

> The discovery that things in his [sic] new surroundings look quite different to what he expected them to be at home is frequently the first shock to the stranger's confidence in the validity of his habitual 'thinking as usual'. Not only the picture which the stranger has brought along of the cultural pattern of the approached group but the whole hitherto unquestioned scheme of interpretation current within the home groups becomes invalidated. It cannot be used as a scheme of orientation within the new social surroundings.

Potentially, therefore, the 'marginal' stranger faces, Janus-like, both the habitual modes of thought and may thus subject them both to quizzical inspection.

I make reference to Schutz here partly in order to characterise my own position as a sranger to this work, and partly to reflect back on my own interests in the sociology of knowledge. In addressing a small number of texts in health economics, therefore, I am interested in using the experience

126

as a pretext for thinking about how we read academic work in general. And what of the phenomenology of reading a strange corpus? My initial impression is that it is indeed a very different experience from reading in one's own academic field, and that such differences help us to reflect on how we use academic texts when we are thinking as usual (to use the phenomenologists' way of characterising everyday practical reasoning).

In the first place, I realise that I have no sense of *authors*. Looking at the list of authors and publications from health economics, I realise that it offers me no clues whatsoever. When I turn to a corpus of sociological writing, especially in my own specialist fields of expertise, then I can normally expect to recognise key names and publications. On that basis I can construct all sorts of assumptions and expectations about the work and the texts (though of course I recognise that those expectations might prove unfounded or incomplete). It is that sense of familiarity that gives me a sense of *authors*. A sense of an author is far more than a name on a series of papers or books. My sense of an author - whether or not known to me personally - is composed out of a variety of items of background knowledge and tacit assumptions. I bring to bear not merely the name of the writer(s), but also what I know about previous publications, general orientations (theoretical and methodological), substantive interests, general reputation, and the like. In other words, the name of the author does not simply index a publication to a writer, it also indexes it to a wider interpretative framework for the competent reader.

For the well-read specialist, moreover, there are many other clues that can be brought to bear on the reading of a specialist text. Important indications and clues are given off from features of the texts themselves, more or less indepndently of their main contents. Extending my sense of authorship, for instance, I can normally inspect the pattern of references and citations in a paper, and glean from that information further important clues about the form and content of the argument in it. Even if an author is not known to me from previous publications, then I can gain a very great deal of insight by inspecting the references in his or her publications. Such information can help to place a publication within a sense of tradition, or within a recognisable 'school of thought'. It is by no means necessary to subscribe to the formal views of bibliometrics and citation analyses to endorse the suggestion that an informal - often cursory - scanning of such information is a routine part of the practical reading of academic work. One might add that seeking out and reading references to one's *own* work is a normal part of inspecting new work in one's own specialist field: we need, perhaps, an academic confessional on such exercises of personal vanity.

In the absence of any such a framework of knowledge and assumptions, I find the strange corpus doubly strange. Not only have I not read it before, but I am deprived of many of the interpretative clues normally available to me when I read in my own subject. Such frameworks of knowledge are not simply aids to lazy reading. They are important in informing the very act of reading itself. They help us to *make* sense of what we read. Contemporary literary theory emphasises the degree to which reading is an active engagement with the text. Texts - literary or academic - do not unequivocally contain and constrain their full 'meanings'. The reader constructs meaning through conventional acts of reading and interpretation. As academics we have our own sense of authorship, of traditions and genres, and the like. We have a pretty shrewd idea of what to expect by way of content, orientation, style and so on. We gain considerable information from the nature of the publication itself. We can often judge something of approach and likely quality from the journal or edited collection in which a paper appears. We can often feel a sense of recognition from the author's academic affilitation. Even the title of a book or article can, in some circumstances at least, give off important messages to the experienced reader. As competent members of a reading community we can rely on an enormous stock of tacit knowledge and assumptions.

Without that sense of genre, authorship and style it can be remarkably difficult to make sense of what one reads. One approaches a text 'cold'. One has no basis on which to pre-judge any aspects of the work in question. And while one might, naively perhaps, expect the academic to approach each new piece of work with an entirely open mind, in reality we do not. We normally have great need of the background assumptions that are furnished by some degree of familiarity: they may be described in terms of genre, paradigm, or tradition. In its absence, one may 'understand' each individual statement, follow the step-by-step logic of each part of an argument, but still find that the overall significance of a publication remains elusive. One can compare the experience to that of the novice student picking his or her way through the prescribed literature (Mann 1974). It sometimes remains remarkably difficult to know quite why *this* author has settled upon *this* topic, tackled it in *this* way, and emphasised *this* aspect of the argument. Readers who are familiar with a discipline and a genre within it will not normally find themselves in the same sort of difficulty. Issues, debates and presuppositions wuill be part of one's taken-for-granted stock of knowledge and will implicitly provide answers for questions about the nature and purpose of an argument or analysis.

Likewise, the novice or strange reader has little or no sense of the development of a discipline, and hence no chronological or sequential framework in which to place a given work. (Dates of publication in isolation are of little help here, I find.) After all, a particular publication may have real significance for the cognoscenti by virtue of its place within a canon of works: because it establishes a new direction for the discipline (apparent in retrospect of course); because it subsequently becomes a *locus classicus* (for better or worse); because it is felt ot be typical or representative of a tendency in the literature; because it is felt to be an oustandingly good example of its sort; because it has pedagogical value; because it is unique or one of very few publications to have dealt with a particular issue. It is not necessary to list all the possible antecedents and outcomes that a well-versed reader may bring to the reading of an academic paper or book. The point is that in the absence of craft knowledge, then the reader encounters academic work in a vacuum. Moreover, it will not necessarily be of help to be told that a given publication is 'typical' of a particular approach, since without knowledge of the relevant genre the reader will not know what feratures make it typical and which are incidental.

These observations are not a complaint about the problems of reading academic work. My point is, rather, that our normal reading of academic literature in our own field rests on thr tacit knowledge owned by the competent member of the relevant academic community. It is such craft knowledge which permeates even the hardest and most precise of laboratory disciplines. Certainly we as sociologists are familiar with such formulations of the craft-knowledge of the academic practitioner, as formulated by C. Wright Mills (1959), for instance. Its acquisition and transmission are largely a matter of apprenticeship, trial-and-error and indeterminate personal skills.

Disciplines in contrast

The exercise of reading health economics was, then, particularly intriguing. I found myself engaged in the juxtaposition of two related but distinct social-science disciplines. To some extent they could be thought of as contrasting paradigms (Kuhn 1962) I use that term somewhat metaphorically here. I am conscious of the fact that the notion of paradigms is problematic in itself, and is particularly so in the context of the social sciences (cf. Barnes 1982). The term is used allusively here, therefore, and yet it does help to convey something about the differences and sitinctions that help demarcate one academic discipline from another.

There are several possible approaches to the contrast or comparison between two or more disciplines. First there is what might be called the *strong incommensurability* position. Such a view would amount to the view that paradigms and disciplines are not directly comparable, but are self-contained and self-justifying somains, each reflecting its own characteristic premises, problems and perspectives. In its strictest version, protagonists of different paradigms would not really be able to agree, disagree or even discuss anything rationally. For strictly speaking they would be talking about differently constucted objects of inquiry. This could lead to complete misunderstanding and failure of comunication if cross-disciplinary contact were attempted. As Moreno and Glassner (1982: 6) suggested:

> The different models lead us to disagree on all counts, so that with regard to any basic principle in one model an advocate of another model will deny that principle.

129

.This seems to be an unnecessarily restrictive and pessimistic view. It seems empirically false, in that our understanding of how scholarship gets done. Scholars can and do shift from one perspective to another; there are areas of constructive dialogue, even if there are many conversations of the deaf as well. Indeed, our experience is surely that some very interesting and important things can happen when you move from one paradigm from another, and that blind incomprehension or mutual hostility are not the only possible outcomes. As I shall suggest in more detail, a strong version of paradigm-mentality can lead researchers and methodologists to over-emphasise the incommensurability of academic traditions and approaches.

A weak - very weak - version of incommensurability is probably true enough, but may lead to an uninteresting conclusion: 'The different models ... sometimes lead us to disagree on some, but not all questions' (Moreno and Glassner 1982: 6). Indeed, if such modest differences were not true, then there would really be no grounds for identifying two or more disciplines or discourses in the first place.

The very opposite if an incommensurability argument would effectively deny the value of any notions such as paradigm. From this perspective, disciplines such as sociology or economics reflect to intrinsic differences. To be sure, the argument would go, they look at different aspects of behaviour, or express different interests. Nonetheless, there is no fundamental difference to be drawn. From this perspective, disciplines address essentially the same phenomena in what is recognisably the same world. Differences in outlook are thus to be seen as acidental rather than essential: epistemological disputes or methodological differences are of little or no interest; different disciplines can, perhaps should, be combined in a fairly unproblematic manner. This sort of response seems equally mistaken. It is based on the view that there exists a body of facts that are entirely independent of the methods used to establish them, and hence of the disciplinary frameworks wherein their significance is formulated. If any scholar actually held to such an extreme, Pollyanna-like view, then he or she would be doing a great disservice to the disciplines involved. Their distinctive assumptions, methods, theories, models - indeed, their characteristic *imagination* - are thereby trivialised.

I therefore want to insist that neither of these extreme positions provides for a reasonable framework for this exercise in cross-disciplinary reading. The first position would, in any case, render the entire exercise irrelevant if not impossible. The strong incommensurability thesis would suggest that nothing useful could be gained by a sociological interrogation of yealth economics or vice versa, and that a shared interest in health, illness and medicine could provide no basis for dialogue. The second position is equally unhelpful for the exercise too. It might lead to the *appearance* of mutual understanding, even of consensus, but it would ultimately frustate the exercide. By denying the importance of methodological or epstemological distinctions, the thesis would close off systematic and serious exploration of disciplinary differences.

The view pursued here, therefore, lies somewhere between the two extremes. In that way one can hope to avoid unproductive conclusions to the exercise of reading a strange corpus. Such unhelpful outcomes would include the view that that the 'other' discipline was entirely irrelevant and held nothing of interest, or that members of the other community were just purblind to the most simple and self-evident of truths. Likewise, one seeks to avoid competitive or imperialist attempts to subordinate or reduce one discourse to the other.

The more fruitful way to approach the problem, I suggest, is to see the two disciplines in a posture of *mutual interrogation*. By this I mean something like the following: as a sociologist reading publications in health economics I am not interested in 'becoming' a health economist nor in pretending to be one. I am not looking to be persuaded to the views of health economists and I do not therefore approach the task of reading as, say, an undergraduate student in the subject might. I do not have to be able to reproduce the discipline myself and I do not therefore have to become fully socialised into its discourse. By the same token, my interest is not in seeking our useful fragments of text that I can use to illustrate and flesh out my own essentially sociological work.

The important work, therefore, in addressing a new corpus would seem to be in a principled exploration of how it is produced as a corpus, sharing discernible ground rules, assumptions, styles, metaphors and the like. Such an inspection cannot be carried out in an intellectual vacuum. It can only be carried out, in part at least, against the background of one's *own* disciplinary allegiances and presuppositions. Hence the importance of a mutual interrogation. such an exercise, when fully realised, should address not only what is said, but also what is unsaid. The silences and the spaces are just as important as what is actually said.

Like the model phenomenologist that I started with, our interest should lie in the taken-for-granted background against which the discourse is constructed: the ways in which phenomena are glossed or glossed over; the kinds of accounts that are offered; the kinds of rhetorical devices that are used to construct the argument. In my own attempted readings I was forced to look beneath the surface of at least some of the economics exemplars. I am not competent (nor I suspect am I constitutionally suited) to the detailed appreciation of, say, a particular utility function. Like the impatient reader of a particular sort of novel I am forced to the equivalent of skipping the author's descriptions and philosophising, preferring to concentrate on the conversations and the action.

As indicated in the introductory paragraphs, this exercise was never intended to yield a thorough review of health economics. In the remainder of this chapter I shall try to illustrate some issues from my highly selective reading. I had no way of knowing whether my reading would prove to be of any direct relevance to the community of health economists' themselves. Like the anthropological stranger I addressed, as a preliminary heuristic, issues that struck me as odd or noteworthy, and issues that recalled familiar problems in a new setting. Rather than doing so on a wide front, in the remainder of the chapter I shall concentrate on a restricted range of closely related topics, In doing so I hope to illuminate the outcome of a stranger's reading and the resulting process of interrogation. In approaching this strange corpus as a sociologist, I find that various representations of social action become a leitmotiv.

Reconstructing social action

One of the topics that strikes the anthropologically naive sociologist as he or she approaches the alien corpus of health economics (or any economics for that matter) relates to the way in which plausible explanations for observed patterns or regularities in action are constructed. Or, to be more precise, attention is likely to be focused on how a given economic model may be related to (often hypothetical) action on the part of actual or ideal-typical social actors.

Let us begin with some examples of text that illustrate what I have in mind here.

> As a basis for the analysis, the assumption is made that each individual acts so as to maximise the expected value of a utility function....
> We presuppose that illness is not a source of satisfaction in itself....
> It is further assumed that individuals are usually risk-averters....
> This assumption may reasonably be taken to hold for most of the significant affairs of life for the majority of people....

These fragments are all taken from Arrow (1973), a key author in the development of health economics as a specialised field of discourse, and relate to his discussion of the particular features of health care that emerge from a distinctively economic perspective. Here the somewhat programmatic nature of the publication itself is a help in this exercise of reading. In a similar vein in Reinhart's discussion of physician productivity (Reinhardt 1972) we find the following suggestions as to the reasons why American physicians have not taken greater advantage of their productivity potential, particularly in relation to the employment of paramedical personnel in greater numbers.

> The physicians themselves may be unaware of the possibilities and potential outcomes.
> Even a well-informed physician may prefer to stay in solo practice and limit the number of staff below the optimum level: he may wish to avoid the extra administrative burden it implies, for instance.

The physican may fear that extensive reliance on paramedical assistants will impair the quality of services provided. (The author adds in a footnote that he knows of no evidence of any 'objective' increase, as would be revealed in an increase of malpractice suits.)
What is described as the physician's 'traditional penchant for privacy and professional independence' is reflected in his attitude towards paramedical employees.

Reinhardt concludes that:

> If one believes that many physians do have a strong preference for a solo practice with few employees, one is finally led to wonder about the factors which have permitted these physicians generally to have been able to maintain their relative income position over time through increases in medical fees. Unfortunately, there has been a strong excess of demand for physician services in recent years. Price changes in the physician sector can therefore readily be substituted for manpower efficiency.

This last extract from Reinhardt illustrates how such inferences about motives for actions, or non-actions, are invoked to account for deviation from the outcomes given by a particular model and the assumption of economic rationality. That model is itself founded on a set of assumptions about motives, intentions and actions, and further assumptions are then added in in order to account for the failure of the original assumptions to account for observed action. I shall comment below on the use of such ironic contrasts and the use of models. For the moment I want to dwell on the nature of the suppositions and hypiotheses cited above, which were selected more or less at random from the selection of published work available to me.

My contention is not that such statements are in themselves illogical, inadmissible, or untrue. Rather, they exemplify how their authors' arguments seem ultimately to rest on the imputation or attribution of motives to the class of actors in question. Moreover, the general methodological principle involved seems to rest on the explanation of social phenomena by reference to the predispositions and preferences of individual actors - actual or ideal. Whether or not these are held to be 'typical' or 'representative' of economic reasoning, the sociological reader who does not tacitly subscribe to the discourse of economics will recognise a version of some very familiar methodological issues. As I see it there are two components to the issue here. First, the extent to which such individualistic explanations are plausible and legitimate. Second, there is the proper way for such explanations to be constructed, if at all.

Now this sort of methodological individualism is thoroughly contested in sociological methodology. But few sociologists would, I suspect, espouse the stonger versions of that, and many would reject it altogether. But rather than offering a reading that recapitulates those old methodological battles, I shall focus on the second aspect of the problem. That is, if we accept individualism for the sake of argument, then how individual action is described and accounted for.

This seems to be an area where mutual interrogation between two epistemic communities might prove illuminating. Modern sociology includes a number of theoretical perspectives of a broadly interpretative kind, drawing on interactionist, phenomenological and ethnomethodological inspirations). They have a number of important doctinal differences, but each in its own way is concerned with understanding and explicating how social actors set about the active accomplishment of everyday life. Social order is seen as the outcome of processes of interactive, collaborative work, and actors are seen as highly adept knowledgeable performers. Their concerted accomplishments are variously characterised in terms of their stocks of knowledge, their members' methods, their shared perspectives, and so forth. Again, the detail of such positions need not detain us here, and we should simply take note of how such theoretical approaches direct attention to everyday life and to actors' commonsense understandings in formulating intentional action. A recognition of the relevance of actors' common sense then directs attention to the analyst's use of his or her *own* common sense in making sense of everyday realities. Classically, ethnomethodologists were particularly concerned with this issue in mounting a radical critique of conventional sociological reasoning. They argued that the latter often rested on the quite unexplicated use of analysts' own commonsense understandings and their own versions of practical reasoning. The implicit assumptions about social action and actors' rationality are introduced, the ethnomethodologists argued, but unacknowledged as explanatory devices in analysts' reconstructions of social action. For the ethnomethodologists and others of a similar persuasion, such everyday knowledge and practical reasoning should not be employed as an unexplicated resource in the inquiry, but should be made the topic of explicit investigation. In other words, such inquiry focuses attention on the characteristics of mundane commonsense reasoning, avoiding reliance on it to interpret social action, or treating it as a residual problem.

Now, to return to our economics examples, it seems that the kind of explanation offered for, say, physician behaviour are analogous to those varieties of sociological reasoning objected to be ethnomethodologists. The analyst, such as Arrow proffers a *plausible* explanation in terms of assumed characteristics, dispositions and actions (or non-actions). Those explanations may or may not be correct representations of dispositions in the real world, but the danger appears to be their invocation in an unprincipled *ad hoc* fashion. Indeed, the contemporary sociologist may feel that he or she does not need the particular strictures of ethnomethodology in order to query the legitimacy of the economists' construction of their hypothetical actors. In the process of mutual interrogation, therefore, the sociologists may find themselves trying to make problematic precisely those features of social action that the economist takes for granted.

The sociologist will want to explore in some detail - and in an empirical fashion - those features of everyday action and belief, those aspects of practical reasoning, that the economist glosses over in the construction of economic arguments and models. Each reading and construction would reflect somewhat different representations of the social actor. Both disciplines are, apparently, equally committed to such issues as choice and value, but such surface similarity masks deeper differences. For the economist, choice is equated with *displayed preference*, which is inferred from observed behaviour. From this perspective, choice and intention are not phenomenological concepts. The sociologist is much less likely to see choice as synonymous with displayed behaviour. He or she is much more likely to point out that what people do, what they say they do, and what they believe may all be quite different; that values and motives will be expressed differently in different contexts; that choice is a highly problematic notions when actors operate in terms of pre-conscious, taken-for-granted stocks of knowledge. While this may in itself be a gross caricature, my reading of the literature suggests that the economist constructs a model actor in the interests of simplicity, while the sociologist is equally interested in the exploration of complexity. That is not a matter of criticism or complacency for either side: the differences reflect the divergent ways in which the respective disciplines construct their subject-matter and their characteristic problems.

These parallels and differences between economic and sociological plausibility can, perhaps, be illustrated in the following ways. First, there is the basic premise of the Pareto approach to welfare economics: Each person is the judge of his or her own welfare. Secondly, there is the sociological axiom of equally classic status: Situations are real insofar as people define them as real and are real in their consequences. I would certainly not wish to claim that these two statements are direct equivalents. Rather, I juxtapose them because they *seem* to have similar implications for their respective disciplines. A decontextualised reading of them could lead one to assume that each provided the same methodological warrant for the detailed explanation of social actors' practical reasoning, modes of rationality and the like.

In practice, however, economists do not appear to treat the Pareto principle as the origin for such analysis. Yet it would surely repay considerable attention. This seems to be indicated by the well-established problem of uncertainty in the economic context. Confusingly, the term is widely used in the sociology of medicine, and to make matters worse, the term is used inconsistently among the sociologists themselves (Atkinson 1995), which should remind us *en passant* of the problems of translation across disciplines. As I understand it from my reading of health economics, the topic of uncertainty is an analytic issue insofar as market models which assume perfect competition equally must assume perfect information. Health care is claimed to be different from such markets, since consumers do not have anything like perfect information. (Indeed, the sociologist might add *sotto voce* that imperfect information is not simply a natural derivation from the division of labour, but is often an active accomplishment in real situations.) Rational decision-making may thus be seen as problematic under conditions of uncertainty. We should note once more that this argument depends heavily on the trope or *irony*, in contrasting the supposed characteristics of 'proper' market conditions with the problematic deviation of health care from that ideal state.

Authors in health economics acknowledge general problems, to be sure, Culyer (1973), for instance, notes a number of issues relating to consumer rationality in the health field:

> Many consumers, though sick, do not desire treatment, and may be ignorant of their sickness.
> The mentally sick do not fit readily into a model of 'consumer sovereignty'.
> Patients requiring emergency treatment are frequently not in a position to reveal their preferences.

Yet these sorts of remarks do not appear to be used to open up the exploration of rationality *per se*. The problem - interestingly for a sociological reader - is expressed in terms of the ignorant, the insane or the incapable. Does this imply that the 'normal' actor can be assumed to act entirely in accordance with the analyst's model of rationality? The sociologist will certainly wish to counter that the implied contrasts - again, irony appears to be a fundamental trope in the economists' arguments - such as rational/irrational, well-informed/ignorant, are too simple actually to characterise social action in a meaningful fashion. Rather, we might want to examine the varieties of rationality that are available; what information actors actually have and how it is distributed; and rather than fretting about perfect information or its absence, inquire what actors would regard as *adequate* information, *warranted* knowledge, and *reasonable* action. It is in that spirit, then, that the sociologist might address the definition of the situation and treat rationality as potentially problematic.

It should be noted that this is *not* proposed as a criticism of economics. Rather, it represents one crucial and revealing difference between the two discipines of sociology and economics, where mutual interrogation helps to throw into relief such divergences. These reflections further help us to scrutinise their respective root metaphors, models and distinctive styles of thought.I have implied that some economic arguments seem to rest on the unexplicated assumption of commonsense and rationality. Now it might be objected by economists that this is far from the truth: that in fact those economic explanations are remarkably *explicit* about their presuppositions. In one sense that would indeed by defensible: such economic arguments are clear about what they assume for the purposes of argument. The sociologist or other outsider may well be struck by the degree to which economists seem to employ clearly specified models. The economist is, after all, inclined to proceed by the construction of a model (such as a market for a particular good; or of an economic decision-maker) by the deployment of a limited number of assumptions and the identification of a limited number of inputs or variables. The approach is portrayed as hypothetico-deductive in style, and the worth of a given model is judged on the basis of its predictive power.

Sociologists are perfectly familiar with these kinds of models and their use, Models of the market, the consumer, the firm and so on are used as heuristic devices, as ideal types against which actual occurrences and observations can be compared. There is often an ironic contrast between such an ideal (e.g. perfect or optimum conditions) and observed states of affairs. Brown (1977) indeed has identified such irony as a pervasive feature of sociological reasoning and writing. Sociologists repeatedly contrast the 'normal' with the 'deviant', only to discover the normality and rationality of deviance; the conventions of particular settings are conrasted with the normality of everyday life; the conventional or mainstream is contrasted with the exotic; the dominant with the muted (Atkinson 1990). The contrasts of latent and manifest functions, or of intended and unintended consequences, provide sociology with its pervasive sense of irony and pathos.

Sociologists, on the other hand, are much less given to attempting to specify ideal-typical models in order to explore the potential or likely outcome of a given change in organization or behaviour. Questions of the form 'What is...?' are not a common feature of the sociologist's stock-in-trade. In part, perhaps, this reflects the sociologist's characteristic reluctance to engage in explicit policy formation. Applied sociology is not a designation - even in policy-relevant areas like medical sociology - that most sociologists themselves would willingly adopt. Social criticism may imply social reconstruction, and indeed social reform is often part of the sociological agenda, but it is not necessarily felt to entail the construction of explicit, hypothetical blueprints.

There is, therefore, a nice irony that becomes apparent here. The health economists are happy to operate with a relatively unproblematic distinction between normative and positive work. They recognise the possibility of a neutral scholarship, only to deploy it for evaluative and prescriptive ends. The sociologists, on the other hand, are for the most part concerned with the inescapably value-laden nature of their enterprise. They have an almost instictive distrust of claims to value-neutrality. Yet they are equally reluctant to engage in prescriptive policy-oriented activity. (They are not reticent in mounting social criticism, but those are rarely framed in systematic programmes of evaluative research.)

This style may be related to sociologists' penchant for making life exquisitely problematic. It may be a source or irritation to non-sociologists in the academy, or to policy-makers, that a common response to any given question or problem is 'Ah, yes, but it isn't as simple as that...'; or 'But you haven't considered...'. The health economist typically asks 'We see that such-and-such is the case...Why...?'. The sociologist is likely to respond 'Such-and-such appears to be the case. But is it?' or 'Contrary to reasonable assumptions...'. The sociologist's apparent reluctance to tackle social problems head on reflects a preoccupation with fundamental preoccupations with method and measurement. The sociologist is all too aware that what he or she measures is itself meaningful to the social actors themselves, and that the social construction of those meanings is not readily - or even properly - translated into the standardised and operationalised measures of positivist science.

Such a sociological sensivity may well be at odds with the economists' agenda, as outlined for instance by Culyer, Lavers and Williams (1971). Those authors propose a scheme for the construction of social indicators, 'designed to achieve the objectives of measuring the quality of life, estimating the effects on social phenomena of the actions of government, commercial and voluntary organizations and of individuals, and measuring the magnitude of social problems, the rate at which these are changing and the manner in which they are inter-related'. It is apparent that if one examines their construction of the state-of-health indicator that the authors are forced, to some extent at least, to gloss over niceties of meaning and measurement. Their appeal is to practical rather than to theoretical concerns:

> Despite the fact that describing the intensity of pain is notoriously difficult, and that interpersonal comparisons are bound to be rather arbitrary due, for example, to varying thresholds of pain, medical personnel can and do make such comparisons between stages and classes of condition, and such comparisons already have to be assimilated into judgements about 'acceptable' degrees of physical disability and pain at the diagnostic and therapeutic level when determining courses of treatment.

The authors therefore go on to propose a ten-point scale of 'intensity of ill-health', ranging from normal through various intermediate stages to dead.

For the sociological observer it might well be of interest to focus on the topic of *how* such judgements (such as acceptable degrees of disability or discomfort) are arrived at, described and legitimated. Likewise, the sociologist should certainly interest himself or herself in the range of personal and social meanings attached to such 'levels' by lay social actors. They might, as a consequence, be much more reticent than the health economists. The latter, on the other hand, make some strong claims for their indicator:

138

> Since it is intended to use these numbers as *weights*, and not simply as *rankings*, it is important to stress that society's judgements concerning the relative importance of avoiding one state rather than another are represented by the actual numbers attached to each respectively, e.g. state 2 is *twice as bad* as state 1, and state 10 is ten times as bad.(emphases in original)

The economists go on to emphasise that this is a policy statement, not a statement of a medical condition. But the scheme does seem to gloss over a wealth of meaning and evaluation, which are certainly not fully covered by the authors' references to 'society's judgements' (however they are arrived at). The sociologist, by contrast, will want to disaggregate the description of 'society's judgements' (and indeed, professionals' judgements) in order to explore the complexity, variablity and situational or practical determinmants of such acts of interpretation.

Again, one draws out the contrast not in order to proclaim the merits of one or other approach. Each has its value. What is interesting, once more, in reading across the disciplines, is the contrast between what is taken for granted or glossed over in each, and what is treated as problematic. Examples of this sort could be repeated extensively, but my aim here is not to produce a detailed point-by-point comparison of the two contrasted disciplines. The point is rather to reflect on the processes and outcomes of such an exercise in academic reading. I shall therefore return to my starting point in the concluding section of this chapter.

Conclusion

The problem for the reader of an alien discipline - and therefore for many readers in general - is the lack of interpretive framework that may be brought to bear on the texts in question. The scholar who is reading in his or her own field does so equipped with a host of tacit assumptions. We often read from a standpoint that implies a particular perspective or attitude. We may embark on a reading expecting to be critical and negative about a given piece of work. We may equally come to a book or paper expecting to be swayed by its arguments and persuaded by its findings. We very often know or know of the author, and feel we know what to expect. We may be able to locate an author and a work in a particular network or clique. We may thus have a framework for approving or sneering. If the work is in our own particular sub-speciality, we may reasonably look for ourselves in the bibliography and look to see whether the citations have been approving or not. We have expectations about the impact and significance of given journals - and hence of their contents - or about particular publishing houses, series editors and the like. We have attitudes about academic departments and research institutes. In other words, we frequently operate with tacit notions of trust and preference. The naive stranger who must encounter a corpus with which he or she has no previous acquaintance has no such supports. He or she has none of those prior expectations. There is no basis for expecting to agree with a piece of work or not. One cannot know whether to agree with an author or not, or whether to approve of a particular method or style of argument. The sense of disorientation is testimony to the power of such normal tacit knowledge.

There are, moreover, tacit expectations about genre and style that inform a normal disciplinary reading of academic texts. The competent reader can bring to bear a host of assumptions concerning the style as well as the content of presentation and argument. This is especially true in when it comes to the characteristic tropes of a given genre. It is very hard to try to read an alien corpus literally, as it were. In the absence of disciplinary background, it can often be difficult to know just how to approach a text. Is it all to be taken literally, for instance, or can it be treated figuratively, as it were? This is an especially pertinent consideration when economics is the discipline in question. As McCloskey (1985) has argued with great vigour, economics in general is shot through with rhetorical devices. Despite its appearance of 'hard' science and rigour, McCloskey argues, economics is highly dependent on tropes of various sorts. Its texts rely thoroughly on narrative and metaphorical usage, for instance. It creates, for example, fables and morality tales: the economist takes a state of affairs and spins hypothetical stories about possible consequences, or how it might have transpired otherwise. Likewise, in the development of models and indicators, the economist uses metaphors and similes. The models and the indicators used to construct them are based on 'as if' analogies and approximations. The economist's use of concepts like 'the market' is essentially metaphorical. It is just as much so as the sociologist's borrowing of terms like 'role' to capture the elements of social performance. Both sets of scholars have become habituated to the figures of speech, to such an extent that their 'as if' character may e all but invisible Nevertheless, as McCloskey argues in the case of economics, the usages are non-literal for all that. The arguments constructed by health economists are thoroughly dependent on similes and metaphors.

The problem for the naive reader is how to approach those essentially metaphorical conventions. Or, to put it in a similar way, just how seriously (literally) should the reader take what he or she reads? When I read of a single indicator for health in which death is given a weighting of ten, I found it hard to know how to take it. The implied statement that death is precisely ten times worse than a state of perfect health seems so absurd to the outsider as to discredit the entire enterprise. Likewise, the models of perfect competition or perfect information seem to distantly related to the complexities of everyday social realities that the naive reader may find it all but impossible to relate such models (metaphors) to real-world phenomena. He or she may then be puzzled as to how, and indeed why, the economist feels able to pontificate on actual policies on the basis of arguments so patently distant from real life. It is, the observer may realise, precisely because the tropes are so unreal that the economist is able to manipulate them (through the construction of equations, for instance) in order to produce his or her predictions. The rhetorical impact of the economists' models (their predictive power) is dependent on the fictive character of their contents. Indeed, the naive reader, who is forced - at least as a first approximation - to read everything literally, may well be struck by the implausibility of the contents of such arguments. Economists' use of indicators is an obvious case in point, where elaborate models may be built on indicators with apparently only shaky validity.

It does not take a naive reader to identify such phenomena, of course. McCloskey is a highly respected economic historian in his own right, and he has been able to identify the essentially rhetorical nature of economic thought and writing. Nevertheless, the experience of reading an alien corpus is a valuable intellectual exercise. It forcibly draws our attention to the phenomenology of reading. It serves to remind us once again that our normal competence as academics is heavily dependent on conventions of tyextual interpretation. Being a sociologist or an economist is closely tied to the ability to read sociology or economics in the appropriate way. Indeed, it is noticeable that in many of the humanities and social sciences, academic socialization is tied to the reading of canonical texts. Those texts are read not just for their specific content, but in order to equip the novice with the appropriate *habitus* (Bourdieu 1988). That is, the tacitly acquired repertoire of habits, preferences and values that comprise the indeterminate and sacred core of disciplinary cultures.

10 Epilogue

This collection of papers has dealt with a diverse range of topics and their composition spans a number of years. Nevertheless, there is a consistent set of preoccupations running through them. Some are recapitulated briefly here.

The main theme of course is that of textuality. When I first embarked on writing about ethnography as text, it was an exhilaratingly lonely exercise. A number of people seemed to be interested, but few were actually engaged in systematic analysis and writing themselves. Within a very few years the position changed markedly. After the publication of a few key texts - notably from cultural anthropologists in the USA - we apparently found ourselves in the throes of yet another intellectual crisis. In this case it was a 'crisis of representation'. The taken-for-granted certainties of reading and writing in the social sciences generally - and in ethnography in particular - seemed to have been undermined so thoroughly that some colleagues found the consequences paralysing. In the absence of consensus and certainty, crisis seemed the only solution that some could contemplate. Some commentators saw my own work as contributing to such a critical moment. It was suggested that in displaying some of the literary conventions of ethnographic reporting one had mounted a powerful critique of ethnography from within.

It was, however, not my intention to undermine the pursuit of ethnography through close attention to its texts. I regard the announcement of a crisis and the consequent loss of confidence as an immature response. It seems to me that we can recognise the conventionality of any and every mode of representation (written or otherwise) without thereeby abandoning the scholarly enterprise altogether. We have long acknowledged that ethnographic research cannot simply hold up a mirror to a social reality that is entirely independent of our modes of inquiry: we must use the resources of language and social action to negotiate and produce our research. In the same way, we must use the available resources to reconstruct social realities in what we write. The right response to vulgar positivism or to vulgar naturalism is not the abandonment of social inquiry altogether, nor the total

142

loss of faith in method. As Hammersley and I argued a long time ago (Hammersley and Atkinson 1983), we need to counter naive versions of epistemology - whatever form they take - by recognising and working with the significance of *reflexivity* in the research process. That is, we need to acknowledge the extent to which our selves and our methods are thoroughly implicated in the processes of research and discovery themselves. We study the social world through social methods. The methods of inquiry are the methods of everyday life themselves. There is, therefore, no need to feel especially threatened by a recognition that we reconstruct versions of the social world through our acts of representation.

Some formulations of the textual perspective have been particularly misleading, it seems to me. In part they have stemmed from a quite proper recognition of the affinities between scholarly and literary work. It is fairly easy to see that the conventions of standard ethnography share many common features with the literary conventions of fiction. The realist novel and the ethnography are both 'compositions'. It is, however, misleading to refer to them both as 'fictions', so as to remove altogether the crucial difference, in that the ethnography is grounded in the systematic investigation of social realities. The conventional, even rhetorical, nature of its textual conventions in no way imply that is should be seen as a fantasy or pure invention. In pursuing this recurrent theme, then, these essays should not be read as part of an anti-scholarly or anti-empirical stance.

It is, therefore, a second and related theme, that a principled understanding of textual conventions of reading and writing should be part of the craft knowledge of scholars. A command of literary conventions should, I believe, be part of the intellectual craftsmanship of social scientists like sociologists and anthropologists. For our collective appreciation of textual convention does not absolve us from requirements of scholarly discipline. On the contrary, the disciplines of scholarship now include those of reading and writing. We need to cultivate a principled exploration of the rhetoric of scholarship as part of the academic socialisation of young scholars, for instance, and any forms of textual experimentation should clearly be accompanied by principled choice and disciplined control over their textual resources. A recognition of textuality and its forms thus imposes new and interesting responsibilities on the social scientist. We have lost our innocence about so many aspects of social life and social analysis. They have now been accompanied by the forms of reading and writing.

As I have tried to indicate in the relevant chapter, moreover, we cannot escape the confines of rhetoric by appealing to personal narrative and confessions. As I have shown, they are just as thoroughly conventional as any other form of scholarly composition. There is thus no escape to some alternative form of 'authenticity' in these personalised narratives. We must avoid the contemporary fashion for narratives of personal experience as the source for an uncontaminated personal voice. There is, of course, no harm in the construction and consumption of personal accounts. But the fact that they are identified as confessional does not mean that they transcend the conventions of genre. Here is a clear example of the intersection of the personal and the cultural through socially shared rhetorical devices and tropes.

It is especially important to recognise that narratives of personal experience in general - not just those of ethnographers' confessionals - are as much compositions as any other mode of representation. In recent years there has been an enormous growth in interest in narratives, lives, (auto)biography and the like. They are undoubtedly important. The analysis of such objects is unquestionably part of the necessary methodological armamentarium of the cultural analyst. On the other hand, there is a perceptible danger that, in some quarters, narratives of personal experience are being celebrated as especially privileged accounts of the self and of lived experience. At a time when the broader narratives of scholarship are felt to be under fire - as in the criticisms scholarship moiunted from the postmodern perspective - the personal narratives of individual lives may take on the appearance of authenticity. While my own discussion of personal narrative is confined to one very particular genre, it is intended to illustrate a more general reservation about the appropriate use of narratives and confessions. The penchant for sociologists and anthropologists to produce such confessions is also, perhaps, symptomatic of a wider cultural tendency - which they should comment on even if they do not contribute to it. That is, a much more general cultural trait of confessional talk and writing. We as social scientists confess and come out to a very small audience. We do so, however, in ways that are reminiscent of a much broader set of styles and genres. The ethnographer's tales of the field are, for example, parallel to many other genres of debunking. They can be likened to various styles of *embarassment* and the revelation of *blunders*. Whether they be television programmes composed of 'out-takes' of actors fluffing their lines, or viewers' videos of family mishaps, the genre feeds on the revelation of momentary incompetence and loss of composure. Those that are based on professionals' lapses are especially telling. The ethnographers' tales of the field have very similar properties and functions. They invite the reader (or the viewer) into a delicious complicity. The gaffes reveal the   professionals in all their vulnerable humanity, and stand in contrast to their polished performances elsewhere (the programme as broadcast, the ethnographic monograph as published). Social scientists need to be aware of what they are doing when they contribute yet further to this cultural phenomenon.

In exploring the conventions of academic writing and reading, much can be learned from a close examination of particular texts, authors and corpuses. We can in particular appreciate how styles of thought and styles of writing are inextricably linked in the construction of a given school of thought, a paradigm or an academic discipline. We can learn from a close reading of familiar texts, and we can also learn from trying to read alien texts and disciplines. In the essays on Goffman and health economics respectively I have tried to illustrate both strategies. In neither case is the intention to provide definitive analyses of the respective subject matter. Rather, I have tried to illustrate through the particular readings the more general value of a textual approach. In other cases, of course, I try to show how the academic substance is carried through particular tropes and rhetorical features. We are thus returned to the general theme of the so-called rhetoric of inquiry. It is imperative that we recognise that scholarly, factual work is inescapably rhetorical. It draws on conventions of representation and argumentation in order to convey plausible arguments to readers or hearers. A recognition of rhetoric is not an abnegation of scientific or scholarly responsibility. The either/or separation of rhetoric from science is an unnecessary and indeed misleading legacy of Enlightenment thinking. Rhetoric has been relegated to the fringes of the social sciences for too long. It is vital that we recognise and celebrate its rightful place.

Bibliography

Agar, M. (1990) Text and fieldwork: Exploring the excluded middle, *Journal of Contemporary Ethnography*, 19, 73-88.

Anderson, E. (1976) *A Place on the Corner*. Chicago: University of Chicago Press.

Armstrong, D. (1983) *Political Anatomy of the Body*. Cambridge: Cambridge University Press.

Arrow, K.J. (1973) The welfare economics of health care. In M.H. Cooper and A.J. Culyer (eds) *Health Economics: Selected Readings*. Harmondsworth: Penguin.

Ashmore, M., Mulkay, M. and Pinch, T. (1989) *Health and Efficiency: A Sociology of Health Economics*. Buckingham: Open University Press.

Atkinson, P.A. (1975) In cold blood: Bedside teaching in a medical school. In G.Chanan and S.Delamont (eds) *Frontiers of Classroom Research*. Slough: National Foundation for Educational Research.

Atkinson, P.A.(1976) *The Clinical Experience: An Ethnography of Medical Education*. Unpublished Ph.D. thesis, University of Edinburgh.

Atkinson, P.A. (1977a) Becoming a hypochondriac. In G.Horobin and A.Davies (eds), *Medical Encounters* . London: Croom Helm.

Atkinson, P.A. (1977b) The reproduction of medical knowledge. In C. Heath, R. Dingwall, M. Reid and M.Stacey (eds) *Health Care and Health Knowledge*. London: Croom Helm.

Atkinson, P.A. (1977c) Professional segmentation and students' experience in a Scottish medical school. *Scottish Journal of Sociology*. 2, 71-85.

Atkinson, P.A. (1981) *The Clinical Experience: The Construction and Reconstruction of Medical Reality*, Farnborough: Gower.

Atkinson, P.A. (1982) Writing ethnography. In H.J. Helle (ed.) *Kultur und Institution*. Berlin: Duncker und Humblot.

Atkinson, P.A. (1984a) Wards and deeds: Taking knowledge and control seriously. In R Burgess (ed.), *The Research Process in Educational Settings: Ten Case Studies*. Lewes: Falmer.

146

Atkinson, P.A. (1984b). Training for certainty, *Social Science and Medicine*, 19, 949-56.

Atkinson, P.A. (1988) Discourse, descriptions and diagnoses: The reproduction of normal medicine. In M. Lock and D. Gordon (eds), *Biomedicine Observed*. Boston: Reidel.

Atkinson, P.A. (1990) *The Ethnographic Imagination: Textual Constructions of Reality*. London and New York: Routledge.

Atkinson, P.A. (1991) Supervising the text, *International Journal of Qualitatiave Studies in Education*, 4, 161-174.

Atkinson, P.A. (1992) *Understanding Ethnographic Texts*. Thousand Oaks: Sage.

Atkinson, P.A. (1994) Rhetoric as skill in a medical setting. In M. Bloor and T. Taraborrelli (eds) *Qualitative Studies in Health and Medicine*. Aldershot: Avebury.

Atkinson, P.A. (1995) *Medical Talk and Medical Work*. London: Sage.

Atkinson, P.A. and Hammersley, M. (1994) Ethnography and participant observation. In N.K. Denzin and Y.S. Lincoln (eds) *Handbook of Qualitative Research*. Thousand Oaks CA: Sage.

Barley, N. (1983) *The Innocent Anthropologist*. London: British Museum Publications.

Barnes, B. (1982) *T.S. Kuhn and Social Science*. London: Macmillan.

Barthes, R. (1979) From work to text. In J.V. Harari (ed.) *Textual Strategies: Perspectives in Post-Structuralist Criticism*. London: Methuen.

Bauman, R. (1986) *Story, Performance, and Event*. Cambridge: Cambridge University Press.

Bazerman, C. (1988) *Shaping Written Knowledge: The Genre and the Activity of the Experimental Article in Science* . Madison: University of Wisconsin Press.

Becker, H.S (1986) *Writing for Social Scientists*. Chicago: University of Chicago Press.

Becker, H.S., Geer, B., Hughes, E.C. & Strauss, A.L. (1961) *Boys in White*. Chicago: University of Chicago Press.

Bell, C. and Encel, S. (eds) (1978) *Inside the Whale*. Oxford: Pergamon.

Bell, C. and Newby, H. (eds) (1977) *Doing Sociological Research*. London: Allen and Unwin.

Bell, C. and Roberts, H. (eds) (1984) *Social Researching*. London: Routledge and Kegan Paul.

Berman, M. (1972) Review of *Relations in Public*, *New York Times Book Review*, 27 February.

Bigus, O.E. (1972) The milkman and his customer: a cultivated relationship, *Urban Life and Culture*, 1, 131-165.

Bluebond-Langner, M. (1980) *The Private Worlds of Dying Children*. Princeton: Princeton University Press.

Blumer, H. (1954) What's wrong with social theory?, *American Sociological Review*, 19, 3-10.

Blumer, H. (1966) Sociological implications of the thought of George Herbert Mead, *American Journal of Sociology*, 71, 535-544.

Blumer, H. (1969) *Symbolic Interactionism*. Englewood Cliffs NJ: Prentice-Hall.

Bogdan, R. and Biklen, S. (1982) *Qualitative Research for Education: An Introduction to Theory and Methods*. Boston: Allyn and Bacon.

Boon, J.A. (1982) *Other Tribes, Other Scribes*. Cambridge: Cambridge University Press.

Boon, J.A. (1983) Functionalists write too: Frazer, Malinowski and the semiotics of the monograph, *Semiotica*, 46, 131-149.

Bosk, C.L. (1979) *Forgive and Remember: The Management of Medical Failure*. Chicago: University of Chicago Press.

Bourdieu. P. (1983) Erving Goffman: Discoverer of the infinitely small, *Theory, Culture and Society*, 2, 112-113.

Bourdieu, P. (1988) *Homo Academicus*. Oxford: Polity.

Bowen, E. (1954) *Return to Laughter*. London: Gollancz.

Brodkey, L. (1987) *Academic Writing as Social Practice*. Philadelphia: Temple University Press.

Brown, R.H. (1977) *A Poetic for Sociology*. Cambridge: Cambridge University Press.

Brown, R.H. (1983) Dialectical irony, literary form and sociological theory, *Poetics Today*, 4, 543-564.

Brunvand, J. (1983) *The Vanishing Hitchhiker*. London: Picador.

Brunvand, J. (1984) *The Choking Doberman*. New York: W.W.Norton.

Brunvand, J. (1985) *The Mexican Pet*. New York: W.W.Norton.

Bruyn, S.T. (1966) *The Human Perspective in Sociology: The Methodology of Participant Observation*. Englewood Cliffs NJ: Prentice-Hall.

Burgess, R.G. (ed.) (1984) *The Research Process in Educational Settings: Ten Case Studies*. London: Falmer.

Burgess, R.G. (ed.) (1985a) *Field Methods in the Study of Education*. London: Falmer.

Burgess, R.G. (ed.) (1985b) *Strategies of Educational Research*. London: Falmer.

Burgess, R.G. (ed.) (1985c) *Issues in Educational Research*. London: Falmer.

Burkett, G. and Knafl. K. (1974). Judgement and decision-making in a surgical specialty, *Sociology of Work and Occupations*, 1, 82-109.

Cappetti, P. (1993) *Writing Chicago: Modernism, Ethnography and the Novel*. New York: Columbia University Press.

Carey, J.T. (1975) *Sociology and Public Affairs: The Chicago School*. Beverly Hills: Sage.

Cicourel, A. (1964) *Method and Measurement in Sociology*. New York: Free Press.

148

Clifford, J. (1978) Hanging up looking glasses at odd corners: Ethnobiographical perspectives, *Harvard English Studies*, 8, 41-56.

Clifford, J. (1981) On ethnographic surrealism, *Comparative Studies in Society and History*, 23, 539-564.

Clifford, J. (1983) On ethnographic authority, *Representations*, 1, 118-146

Clifford, J. and Marcus, G.E. (eds.), (1986). *Writing Culture: The Poetics and Politics of Ethnography*. Berkeley: University of California Press.

Clough, P.T. (1992) *The End(s) of Ethnography: From Realism to Social Criticism*. Newbury Park: Sage.

Coffey, A. and Atkinson, P.A. (1995) Realism and its discontents. In B. Adam and S. Allen (eds) *Theorizing Culture*. London: UCL Press.

Comaroff, J. (1982) Medicine: Symbol and ideology. In P. Wright and A. Treacher (eds) *The Problem of Medical Knowledge*. Edinburgh: Edinburgh University Press.

Coward, R. and Ellis, J. (1977) *Language and Materialism: Developments in Semiology and the Theory of the Subject*. London: Routledge and Kegan Paul.

Cowley, M. (1950) A natural history of American naturalism. In S. Persons (ed.) *Evolutionary Thought in Ameria*. New Haven, Conn.: Yale University Press.

Crapanzano, V. (1977) The writing of ethnography, *Dialectical Anthropology*, 2, 69-73.

Culyer, A.J. (1973) Is medical care different? In M.H. Cooper and A.J. Culyer (eds) *Health Economics: Selected Readings*. Harmondsworth: Penguin.

Culyer, A.J., Lavers, R.J. and Williams, A. (1971) Social indicators: Health, *Social Trends*, 2, 31-41.

Danto, A.C. (1985) *Narration and Knowledge*. New York: Columbia University Press.

Delamont, S. (1989) The nun in the toilet, *International Journal of Qualitative Studies in Education*, 2, 191-202.

Delamont, S. (1991) The HIT LIST and other horror stories: sex roles and school transfer, *The Sociological Review*, 39, 238-259.

Delamont, S. and Atkinson, P. (1995) *Fighting Familiarity*. New York: Hampton Press.

Denzin, N. and Keller, C. (1981) Frame analysis reconsidered, *Contemporary Sociology*, 10, 52-60.

Dey, I. (1995) Reducing fragmentation in qualitative research. In U. Kelle (ed.) *Computer-Aided Qualitative Data Analysis*. London: Sage.

Dingwall, R. (1976) *Aspects of Illness*. London: Martin Robertson.

Dingwall, R. (1977), 'Atrocity stories' and professional relationships, *Sociology of Work and Occupations*, 4, 371-96.

Duneier, M. (1992) *Slim's Table: Race, Respectability and Masculinity*. Chicago: University of Chicago Press.

Edmondson, R. (1984) *The Rhetoric of Sociology*. London: Macmillan.

Erikson, K. (1976) *Everything in its Path*. New York: Simon and Schuster.

Fabian, J. (1983) *Time and the Other: How Anthropology Makes Its Object*. New York: Columbia University Press.

Fardon, R. (ed.) *Localizing Stategies: Regional Traditions of Ethnographic Writing*. Edinburgh: Scottish Academic Press.

Faris, R.E.L. (1970) *Chicago Sociology 1920-1932*. Chicago: University of Chicago Press.

Fetterman, D. (ed.) (1984) *Ethnography in Educational Evaluation*. Beverly Hills: Sage.

Fine, G.A. and Martin, D.D. (1995) Humor in ethnographic writing: Sarcasm, satire, and irony as voices in Erving Goffman's *Asylums*. In J. Van Maanen (ed.) *Representation in Ethnography*. Thousand Oaks CA: Sage.

Fisher, S. and Todd, A. (eds) (1983) *The Social Organization of Doctor-Patient Communication*. Washington DC: Center for Applied Linguistics.

Fleck, L. (1979) *Genesis and Development of a Scientific Fact*. Chicago: University of Chicago Press.

Foucault, M. (1976) *Birth of the Clinic*. London: Tavistock.

Fox, N.J. (1991) *The Social Meaning of Surgery*. Buckingham: Open University Press.

Friedl, E. (1962) *Vasilika: A Village in Modern Greece*. New York: Holt, Rinehart and Winston.

Geer, B. (1964) First days in the field. In P. Hammond (ed.) *Sociologists at Work*. New York: Basic Books.

Geertz, C. (1983) Slide show: Evans-Pritchard's African transparencies, *Raritan*, 3, 62-80.

Geertz, G. (1988) *Works and Lives: The Anthropologist as Author*. Cambridge: Polity.

Glaser, B, and Strauss, A.L. (1967) *The Discovery of Grounded Theory*. Chcago: Aldine.

Goffman, E. (1971) *The Presentation of Self in Everyday Life*. Harmondsworth: Penguin.

Goffman, E. (1972) *Relations in Public*. Harmondsworth: Penguin.

Goffman, E. (1975) *Frame Analysis*. Harmondsworth: Penguin.

Goffman, E. (1981) Reply to Denzin and Keller, *Contemporary Sociology*, 10, 60-68.

Halbwachs, M. (1992) *On Collective Memory*. Chicago: University of Chicago Press.

Hammersley, M. (1991) *Reading Ethnographic Research: A Critical Guide*. London: Longmans.

Hammersley, M. and Atkinson, P. (1983) *Ethnography: Principles in Practice*. 1st ed. London: Tavistock.

Hammersley, M. and Atkinson, P. (1995) *Ethnography: Principles in Practice*. Second ed. London: Routledge.

Hammond, P. (ed.) (1964) *Sociologists at Work*. New York: Basic Books.

Hannerz, U. (1969) *Soulside*. New York: Columbia University Press.

Hargreaves, A. (1981) Contrastive rhetoric and extremist talk. In L. Barton and P. Woods (eds), *Schools, Teachers and Teaching*. Milton Keynes, Open University Press.

Harvey L. (1987) *Myths of the Chicago School of Sociology*. Aldershot: Avebury.

Heath, C. C. (1986), *Body Movement and Speech in Medical Interaction*. Cambridge: Cambridge University Press.

Herzfeld, M. (1982) *Ours Once More*. Austin: University of Texas Press.

Herzfeld, M. (1985) *The Poetics of Manhood*. Princeton: Princeton University Press.

Horobin, G. and Davis, A. (eds) (1977) *Medical Encounters*. London: Croom Helm.

Hughes, D. (1976) Everyday and medical knowledge in categorising patients. In R. Dingwall, C. Heath, M.E. Reid and M. Stacey (eds) *Health Care and Health Knowledge*. London: Croom Helm

Jackson, J.E. (1990) Deja entendu: The liminal qualities of anthropological fieldnotes, *Journal of Contemporary Ethnography*, 19, 8-43

Jacobs, G. (ed.) (1970) *The Participant Observer*. New York: Braziller.

Katz, P. (1984) Ritual in the operating room., *Ethnology*, 20, 330-350.

Katz, P. (1985) How surgeons make decisions. In R.A.Hahn and A.D.Gaines (eds.) *Physicians of Western Medicine: Anthropological Approaches to Theory and Practice*. Boston: Reidel.

Kenna, M. (1990) Family and economic life in a Greek island community. In C.C. Harris (ed.) *Family, Economy and Community*. Cardiff: University of Wales Press.

Kleinman, A. (1988) *The Illness Narratives: Suffering, Healing and the Human Condition*. New York: Basic Books.

Knafl, K. and Burkett, G. (1975) Professional socialization in a surgical specialty: Acquiring medical judgement, *Social Science and Medicine*, 11, 477-484.

Krieger, S. (1979) Research and the construction of a text. In N. Denzin (Ed.) *Studies in Symbolic Interaction Vol. 2*. Greenwich, Conn.: JAI Press.

Krieger, S. (1983) *The Mirror Dance: Identity in a Women's Community*. Philadelphia: Temple University Press.

Krieger, S. (1984) Fiction and social science. In N. Denzin (ed.) *Studies in Symbolic Interaction, Vol. 5*. Greenwich, Conn.: JAI Press.

Kuhn, T.S. (1962) *The Structure of Scientific Revolutions*. Chicago: University of Chicago Press.

Labov, W. (1972) The transformation of experience in narrative syntax. In W. Labov, *Language in the Inner City*. Philadelphia: University of Pennsylvania, Press.

Labov, W. and Waletsky, J. (1967) Narrative analysis: Oral versions of personal experience. In J Helm (ed.), *Essays on the Verbal and Visual Arts*. Seattle: University of Washington Press.

Law, J. and Williams, R.J. (1982) Putting the facts together: A case study of scientific persuasion, *Social Studies of Science*, 12, 535-558.

Le Baron, C. (1982) *Gentle Vengeance*. New York: Penguin.

Lederman, R. (1990). Pretexts for ethnography: On reading fieldnotes. In R. Sanjek (ed.) *Fieldnotes: The Makings of Anthropology*. Ithaca NY: Cornell University Press.

Liebow, E. (1967) *Tally's Corner, Washington DC: A Study of Negro Streetcorner Men*. Boston: Little, Brown

Lightfoot, S.L. (1983) *The Good High School*. New York: Basic Books.

Lodge, D. (1977) *The Modes of Modern Writing*. London: Edward Arnold.

Lofland, J. (1971) *Analyzing Social Settings*. Belmont CA: Wadsworth.

Lofland, J. (1974) Styles of reporting qualitative field research, *American Sociologist*, 9, 101-111.

Lofland, J. (1980) Early Goffman: style, structure, substance, soul. In J. Ditton (ed.) *The View from Goffman* (pp. 24-51). London: Macmillan.

Lurie, A. (1978) *Imaginary Friends*. Harmondsworth: Penguin.

Lutkehuas, N. (1990) Refractions of reality: On the use of other ethnographers' fieldnotes. In R. Sanjek (ed.), *Fieldnotes: The Makings of Anthropology*. Ithaca NY: Cornell University Press.

Mann, P.H. (1974) *Students and Books*. London: Routledge and Kegan Paul.

Manning. P.K. (1976) The decline of civility: A comment on Erving Goffman's sociology, *Canadian Review of Sociology and anthropology*, 13, 13-25.

Marcus, G.E. (1980) Rhetoric and the ethnographic genre in anthropological research, *Current Anthropology*, 21, 507-510.

Marcus, G.E. and Cushman, D. (1982) Ethnographies as texts, *Annual Review of Anthropology*, 11, 25-69.

Mascia-Less, F.E., Sharpe, P. and Cohen, C.B. (1989) The postmodernist turn in anthropology: Cautions from a feminist perspective, *Signs*, 15, 7-33.

McCloskey, D.N. (1985) *The Rhetoric of Economics*. Madison: University of Wisconsin Press.

McKeganey, N. and Cunningham-Burley, S. (eds.) (1988) *Enter the Sociologist*. Aldershot: Gower.

Messerschmidt, D.S. (ed.) (1982) *Anthropologists at Home in North America*. New York: Cambridge University Press.

Mills, C.W. (1959) *The Sociological Imagination*. London: Oxford University Press.

Mishler, E. (1984) *The Discourse of Medicine: Dialectics of Medical Interviews*, Norwood, NJ: Ablex.

Moreno, J.D. and Glassner, B. (1982) *Discourse in the Social Sciences*. Westport, Conn.: Greenwood.

Mulkay, M. (1985) *The Word and the World*. London: George Allen and Unwin.

Murcott, A. (1981) On the typification of 'bad' patients. In P. Atkinson and C. Heath (eds) *Medical Work: Realities and Routines*. Aldershot: Gower.

Myers, G. (1990) *Writing Biology: Texts in the Social Construction of Scientific Knowedge*. Madison: University of Wisconsin Press.

Parker, R.B. (1982) *Looking for Rachel Wallace*. London: Piatkus.

Pithouse, A. (1985) Poor visibility: Case talk and collegial assessment in a social work office, *Work and Occupations*, 12, 77-89.

Pithouse, A and Atkinson, P (1988) Telling the case: occupational narrative in a social work office, in N. Coupland (ed.) *Styles of Discourse*. London: Croom Helm.

Posner, T. (1976) Magical elements in orthodox medicine. In R. Dingwall, C. Heath, M.E. Reid and M. Stacey (eds) *Health Care and Health Knowledge*. London: Croom Helm.

Propp, V. (1968) *Morphology of the Folktale*. Austin: University of Texas Press.

Reinhardt, U.E. (1972) A product function for physician services, *Review of Economics and Statistics*, 54, 55-67.

Reynolds, L.T. and Meltzer, B.N. (1973) The origins of divergent methodological stances in symbolic interactionism, *The Sociological Quarterly*, 14, 189-199.

Richardson, L. (1990) *Writing Strategies*. Newbury Park: Sage.

Rock, P. (1979) *The Making of Symbolic Interactionism*. London: Macmillan.

Rosenberg, H.G. (1988) *A Negotiated World: Three Centuries of Change in a French Alpine Community*. Toronto: University of Toronto Press.

Roustang, F. (1983) *Psychoanalysis Never Lets Go*. Baltimore: Johns Hopkins University Press.

Said, E. (1978) *Orientalism*. New York: Pantheon.

Sanjek, R. (Ed.) (1990) *Fieldnotes: The Makings of Anthropology*. Ithaca: Cornell University Press.

Schatzman, L. and Strauss, A.L. (1955) Social class and modes of communication, *American Journal of Sociology*, 60, 329-38.

Schutz, A. (1964) The stranger. In *Collected Papers Vol. 2*. The Hague: Martinus Nijhoff.

Schutz, A. (1967) *The Phenomenology of the Social World*. Chicago: Northwestern University Press.

Scott, M.B. (1968) *The Racing Game*. Chicago: Aldine.

Shem, S. (1978) *The House of God*. New York: Dell.

Silverman, D (1987) *Communication and Medical Practice: Social Relations in the Clinic*. London and Beverley Hills: Sage.

Smith, D. (1987) *The Everyday World as Problematic*. Boston: Northeastern University Press.

Sontag, S (1966) The anthropologist as hero. In E.N. Hayes and T. Hayes (eds) *Claude Levi-Strauss: The Anthropologist as Hero.*

Spencer, J. (1989) Anthropology as a kind of writing, *Man*, 24, 45-64.

Spindler, G. (ed.) (1982) *Doing the Ethnography of Schooling.* New York: Holt, Rinehart and Winston.

Stanley, L. and Wise, S. (1983) *Breaking Out: Feminist Consciousness and Feminist Research.* London: Routledge and Kegan Paul.

Strong, P. (1980) Doctors and dirty work - the case of alcoholism, *Sociology of Health and Illness*, 2, .24-47.

Tesch, R. (1990) *Qualitative Research: Analysis Types and Software Tools.* London: Falmer.

Tyler, S.A. (1986) Post-modern ethnography: from document of the occult to occult document. In J. Clifford and G. Marcus (eds) *Writing Culture: The Poetics and Politics of Ethnography.* Berkeley: University of California Press.

Van Maanen, J. (1988) *Tales of the Field.* Chicago: University of Chicago Press.

Walford, G. (ed.) (1988) *Doing the Sociology of Education.* London: Routledge.

Weaver, A. and Atkinson, P.A. (1994) *Microcomputing and Qualitative Data Analysis.* Aldershot: Avebury.

West, C. (1984) *Routine Complications: Troubles With Talk Between Doctors and Patients.* Bloomington: Indiana University Press.

White, H. (1973) *Metahistory: The Historical Imagination in Nineteenth Century in Europe.* Baltimore: Johns Hopkins University Press.

Whyte, W.F. (1981) *Street Corner Society: The Social Structure of an Italian Slum.* Third edn.. Chicago; University of Chicago Press (First edn 1955).

Whyte, W.F. (1985) *Learning from the Field.* Beverly Hills: Sage.

Williams, R. (1976) Symbolic interactionism: the fusion of theory and research? In D.C. Thorne (ed.) *New Directions in Sociology.* London: David and Charles.

Williams, R. (1983) Sociological tropes, *Theory, Culture and Society*, 2, 99-102.

Wolcott, H. (1990) *Writing Up Qualitative Research.* Newbury Park: Sage

Wolf, D.R. (1991) High-risk methodology: reflections on leaving an outlaw society. In W.B. Shaffir and R.A. Stebbins (eds) *Experiencing Fieldwork: an Inside View of Qualitative Research.* Newbury Park CA: Sage.

Wolf, M. (1992) *A Thrice Told Tale: Feminism, Postmodernism and Ethnographic Responsibility.* Stanford CA: Stanford University Press.

Woolgar, S. (ed.) (1988) *Knowledge and Reflexivity: New Frontiers in the Sociology of Knowledge.* Beverly Hills: Sage.

Wright, W. (1975) *Sixguns and Society: A Structural Study of the Western.* Berkeley: University of California Press.

Yearley, S. (1981) Textual persuasion: the role of social accounting in the construction of scientific arguments, *Philosophy of Social Science*, 11, 409-435.

For Product Safety Concerns and Information please contact our EU
representative GPSR@taylorandfrancis.com
Taylor & Francis Verlag GmbH, Kaufingerstraße 24, 80331 München, Germany

www.ingramcontent.com/pod-product-compliance
Lightning Source LLC
Chambersburg PA
CBHW050527270326
41926CB00015B/3105